# Weird Bristol

## CHARLIE REVELLE-SMITH

*For my parents.*

*This book would not have been possible if they had not taught me the simple pleasure of a walk, and to always have an inquisitive mind.*

# Introduction: What Does it Mean to be Weird?

Well? What *does* it mean?

When I first started working on the Weird Bristol Twitter feed back in February of 2017, I thought I had a pretty fixed idea of what the concept meant, but the longer it has gone on, I've come to appreciate just what an intangible quality weirdness is…

The Weird Bristol project started as little more than an afterthought. I'd been working on my *Bristol Murders* series of novels and books two and three drew quite heavily on lesser-known aspects of Bristol's history. I found that over time, I'd inadvertently accrued a small library of trivia concerning the city's past and was certain that I couldn't be the only person to find this information interesting, so one morning I headed out with my camera and started snapping away at the little curios I thought revealed some of our city's more unusual secrets.

It turns out that I was right - there was quite an appetite for these bite-sized servings of Bristol history and over time, I started to wonder if I should assemble some of these nuggets into something more permanent and detailed. This book is the result.

Right from the very start, my definition of what qualified as "weird" was a very loose one. Some things like ghostly hauntings or alien encounters fit the brief very neatly, but so do the answers to questions like "why does the Exchange Building clock have two minute hands" and "why are there iron edges to the pavements?" Soon, "weird" was such a broad term that I was sharing stories of unsung heroes of our city's past - as well as some of its forgotten villains too, along with the trivia behind some of our most popular buildings.

So what does the weird in Weird Bristol mean? I've concluded that it can be anything that's not the standard history of the city. It is the lesser-known and hidden story told through artifacts of the past. In writing this book, I discovered that by assembling all these pieces together, somehow a larger portrait of our city was being painted in a way which I hope is unique.

Suddenly it was clear why the construction of the Floating Harbour resulted in a cholera outbreak in south Bristol and how the city's role in the English Civil War led to our oldest statue being decapitated.

On another level, my goals have been much smaller. Every day we all pass oddities without giving them so much as a second thought - be it the little statue of a dog on a Park Row building or the tree on the Downs which is annually painted white. I hope that in sharing a little piece of trivia about these curios, followers of my feed or readers of this book might have a better understanding of our fascinating history and not take those relics from our past for granted.

Or at the very least, they might think, "I never knew that. How weird!"

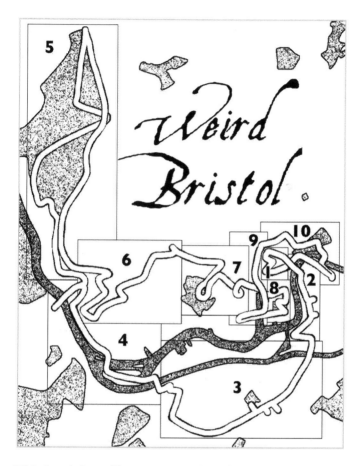

This book is unlike most you'll find about Bristol history, in that there's many different ways of reading it.

Each chapter in this book is referred to as a walk and focuses on a different (sometimes loosely defined) area of the city. Each of the ten walks has ten stops along the way where historic oddities can be found, followed by instructions on how to get to the next location. Each walk also begins with a map to help you track down where these locations are.

The walks range from very simple, such as the ones around Old Town and Queen Square, to quite challenging, such as the ones concerning Hotwells and the Downs. Depending on your abilities, you can do as many as you want in a row as each walk begins close to where the previous one finished.

In fact, if you were to attempt all ten walks in a single go, you'll find that the final walk concludes at the start of the first, as the entire book takes you on one enormous loop around the city!

Alternatively, of course, you don't have to head out the door at all, and this book can be simply enjoyed from the comfort of your home. It doesn't even have to be read from cover-to-cover, so feel free to dip in and out wherever you want to. Not interested in statues? Perhaps some haunted pubs will be more to your taste. No time for pirates? Here are some stories of Bristol Suffragettes!

However you choose to read this book, I hope you enjoy it and above all else, I hope it gives you a greater understanding of this thrilling, wondrous and of course, weird city we call our home.

# Walk One
## Old Town

# Old Town

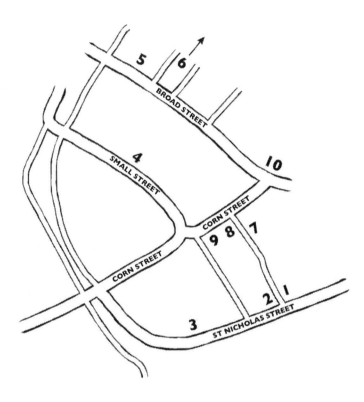

Our first adventure into the hidden history of Bristol will take us through Old Town, a place which, as its name suggests, has seen more than its fair share of historic events. We shall discover grave robbers, find the church at the heart of the bubonic plague epidemic and may even get a glimpse of death herself...

Our journey begins on St Nicholas Street, at the location marked "1" on the map.

# 1. The Queen Victoria Drinking Fountain.

Tucked away behind St Nicholas Market, this seldom-seen drinking fountain bearing the likeness of Queen Victoria is one of our city's neglected treasures, with a fascinating, yet almost forgotten history of its own.

Built in 1859, poor Victoria has spent much of the previous few decades staring at the back of an assortment of wheelie bins, as this section of St Nicholas Street has fallen somewhat into disuse. However, in its day, this fountain was meant to be the start of a revolution.

During the mid 1850s temperance societies were founded across the UK in an attempt to battle what was seen as the scourge of alcohol across the nation, particularly in our cities, where booze - most prominently the dreaded gin - was blamed for the downfall of modern Britain as urban centres became increasingly viewed as drunken and depraved hellholes where traditional values had given way to vice.

To counter this assault on Victorian ethics, these temperance societies suggested installing drinking fountains across cities to offer people a free alternative to drinking alcohol. Five such fountains were built in central Bristol with this example being the only one to survive intact from that era.

It's believed that Queen Victoria's stern countenance was to remind passersby of the principles of Queen and Country and that Britain had been founded upon restraint and dignity. There was also a persistent rumour, no doubt encouraged by temperance societies, that Queen Victoria herself abstained from alcohol of any kind, a rumour we now know to be completely untrue as in fact the queen spent most of her reign, from morning to night, slightly inebriated.

One of the biggest supporters - and financial backers of the Bristol temperance societies, was Henry Overton Wills, the tobacco importer who manufactured cigarettes across the city.

The Wills family were Quakers, a religious organisation long known for its affiliations with radical and progressive causes and as such, saw alcohol as the downfall of the working man. This simple act of offering an alternative to booze was, in its own way, a rather revolutionary one, hoping to inspire people with a different way to live - one without the perils of intoxicating liquors and its associated dependency.

Henry Wills also contributed a large sum of money to help build the Bristol Commercial Coffee Rooms on Corn Street, an establishment to rival those in London which had been founded as a substitute for pubs, offering coffee instead of alcohol. It is now known simply as the Commercial Rooms - a rather stark contrast to the sobriety and restraint its founders had in mind.

Though temperance societies experienced mixed success, this solitary and rather beautiful fountain is testament to the attempts of a group of people who believed Britain could and should strive to be better - and also a reminder that though many individuals throughout history have tried to steer us away from alcohol, it takes quite some effort to get the British to give up their booze.

*From here it's a quick stroll to 18 St Nicholas Street.*

## 2. The Mysterious Veiled Lady

A hairdressing salon may not seem a likely location for one of our city's most enduring mysteries, but ever since a row of heads lining the strip above the doors was built in 1869, people have found something eerie and enigmatic about one of the figures.

Three of the four heads are believed to represent men, the one at the furthest right is most likely an old man whose beard appears to be caught in a strong gust of wind, whilst the figure next to him, face obscured by a veil, is presumed to be a woman.

The row of heads was designed by sculptor Archibald Pontin and architect William Venn Gough, though it has been noted that the veiled lady bears a striking resemblance to a bust created by Italian sculptor Raffaelle Monti, who, while exiled in London, carved a beguiling, veiled woman. His sculpture, now in the possession of Chatsworth House is believed to have inspired Pontin and Venn Gough when they set about designing the ornate facade of this building, which was to be at the time of opening, a pharmacy.

There are two widely believed theories to explain what this row of heads signifies, the most commonly suggested is that they represent the four seasons, with the two young men on the left as spring and summer, the veiled woman as autumn and the old man as winter. Alternatively, it is believed by some that they are the four ages of man, with the veiled "lady" either being another man in somewhat unlikely attire or even that she was there as a kind of mid-Victorian attempt at diverse representation.

There is however, a third theory as to who she may represent, and it's a fascinatingly morbid one. Raffaelle Monti's original sculpture has been alleged to represent an extremely rare example of Death in the form of a woman - and is one of only a handful believed to do so. It's been theorised that Pontin and Venn Gough were providing their own commentary about 19th Century healthcare by depicting three figures attempting to prolong the inevitability of death via the services of an apothecary, all the while death herself waits in their presence for her time to come. We may even be expected to surmise that she may have just claimed a victim - the fourth man whose place she now occupies.

Whoever she is, or whatever she may represent, the Veiled Lady had held a mysterious power over Bristol

14

for the past 150 years. It's hard to look at her unsettling visage and not feel an eerie shudder that something just isn't right about her. Though people have tried to discover her secrets, it seems she would rather keep them to herself…

*It's another short walk to our next stop, 32 St Nicholas Street.*

### 3. The Radnor Hotel - Bristol's First Gay Bar

32 St Nicholas Street is currently Mr Wolfs, a much loved and intimate music venue, but in its earlier life this building was the first of a kind.

From when it opened sometime around 1925, it was home to the Radnor Hotel, discretely operating as the first pub in Bristol to cater for an LGBT+ clientele (lesbian, gay, bisexual, trans and others).

The early years of the Radnor are shrouded in mystery, which is no surprise considering it opened about 40 years before homosexual acts were decriminalised in England and Wales, but it is known that it was licensed to a husband and wife and that the narrow space also offered rooms upstairs which could by rented for the night, should the patrons of the pub need a discreet place to spend some time.

Its role as a gay pub was kept mostly a secret and it had a kind of dual life; by day it proved a popular haunt of market tradesmen and city workers but by night the curtains were drawn, the lights were dimmed and a different clientele, from all across the city, were able to experience a place many of them would come to think of as a second home.

Many of the patrons were theatre workers and performers but for much of the mid 20th century it was popular with sailors who would discretely pass through its doors and into a world populated with drag queens (including an early appearance by Danny La Rue) and a succession of no-nonsense landladies who ruled over the pub with a brash authority.

Though its full identity remained a mystery to most in Bristol, during WWII word soon spread through the ranks of American soldiers stationed in the city as to just what the nature of the Radnor was and the pub was soon host to a handful of Americans who brought with them strange new words such as "gay" as opposed to "queer" to refer to homosexuals - which may be the first known incidence of "gay" being used in that context in Britain.

With the decriminalisation of homosexuality in 1967, the Radnor was able to "come out of the closet" and soon took on a reputation as something of a den of sin among locals, but the clientele seem to have been mostly left in peace. By the early 1970s it was so popular that it was near impossible to get in after 9pm.

However, by 1975 more LGBT+ venues had opened across the city and the Radnor struggled to maintain its regulars, the Elephant, a markedly more wholesome bar, opened a few doors down and the Radnor closed soon afterwards.

In less than a century since the Radnor first opened its doors, attitudes (and the law) in Britain have changed so radically that it's hard to imagine just what a safe haven places such as this must once have been. Now Bristol can pride itself on being home to all walks of life from across the country who no longer have to live secret lives or ones lived in fear.

*Follow St Nicholas Street around the corner to Corn Street and then onto Small Street. The building we're interested in is the Guildhall, the large building opposite Bristol Crown Court.*

# 4. Richard Amerike - America's True Namesake?

The ornate but somewhat dilapidated building on Small Street is the Guildhall Building, an 1840s built meeting place for members of various merchant guilds. Weavers who have had a presence in this area for many centuries would have met here, and later, printers and typesetters.

On the exterior of the building there are a few stone shields bearing coats of arms, the furthest left of which features three stars and six vertical bands. This is the coat of arms of the Amerike family, most prominent of whom was Richard Amerike.

Richard was born in Wales in 1440 but came to Bristol to make his fortune. As a wealthy merchant, it is believed that he endowed John Cabot's journey to the New World with a healthy sum of money.

Cabot's 1497 voyage from Bristol across the Atlantic in the ship "The Matthew" resulted in him being the first European known to have set foot on the American continent.

Further rumours have suggested that Cabot was so touched by Amerike's generosity that he decided to name the land after his benefactor, and thus America came to bear the name of a Bristol merchant.

Some have even suggested that the American flag is an elaborate interpretation of the Amerike coat of arms, though this seems to be a stretch of the imagination as Old Glory was designed centuries after Richard Amerike had died, and furthermore, it doesn't look anything like the Amerike coat of arms - at all.

Most Americans themselves will inform you that their continent is named after the Italian explorer Amerigo Verspucci, and most historians agree that this is the most likely root of the word, however, there remain persistent questions such as why, when almost every city, country and continent named after a person chooses to use the surname rather than first name of that person, would America not be named Verspuccia, and why did Verspucci only start telling people America was named after him several years after the continent had began colonisation?

It would seem to be evidence in favour of our Bristolian merchant but unfortunately not. The theory was first put forward by local historian Alfred Hudd in 1908 and was subsequently elaborated and romanticised. Hudd seems to have offered his theory merely as a possibility and provided no hard evidence to substantiate his claims. Moreover, there isn't any proof that Amerike paid any money at all to aid Cabot's crossing and the two men most likely never had any meaningful contact with each other.

While the evidence for Richard Amerike being America's namesake might be a bit shaky, it seems to be about as firm as it is for Amerigo Verspucci. So could America be named after a Bristol tradesman?

It's possible…

*From here you can pass through the walkway at the lower end of Small Street to connect with Broad Street. It can be quite dark and squalid along there so you may prefer to retrace your steps to Corn Street and join Broad Street there. Either way, our next location is the breathtaking Edward Everard building at 37-38 Broad Street.*

## 5. The Everard's Printing Works

If you want to see people stunned by beauty, spend a few minutes hanging around by the Everard's Printing Works on Broad Street and it won't be long until somebody walks by and catches sight of this hidden marvel of Bristol architecture for the very first time.

Building began on this wonder back in 1900 to a design by Henry Williams and was completed the following year to much confusion in the local press from people who could not agree if it was a thing of beauty or an out of place eyesore. Bristol was experiencing its first brush with Art Nouveau and was unsure what to make of it.

Art Nouveau was a style of architecture and, more generally, art which was enormously popular for about twenty years, beginning in 1890. The style was seen as a celebration of natural forms, particularly of plants and flowers, and gleefully did away with the straight lines and uniform symmetry that had dominated much of the previous two centuries. It was also a reaction to a certain style of Victorian art which had begun to seem too stuffy and formal, and as a new century approached a concerted effort was made across Europe to find a style which would define the 20th century.

The facade is made of Carrara marble tiles, each of which has been hand painted. It is the largest decorative facade of its kind in Britain.

Though the outline of the building is somewhat reminiscent of the nearby Church of St John the Baptist, built into the Old City wall, this is not a monument to a god but to knowledge. The building was originally used as a factory for printing newspapers and books, and as such, the exterior celebrates the printed word, with the female figure at the top of the building an embodiment of the light and truth to be found in literature, whilst the two men are print pioneers William Morris and Johannes Gutenberg (each with an example of the typefaces they would have used.)

Despite much of the interior being stripped away or demolished in 1970 before being converted into a bank ( soon to be converted again into a luxury hotel) the exterior has been preserved as it originally was and now the Everard's Printing Works is one of the best loved buildings in the city and a hidden gem that has for a century, taken breaths away

*Our next stop is through St John's Lane, a narrow road a little to the right of Everard's building. Follow the lane to a low wall, beyond which is a small cemetery behind an iron fence.*

## 6. The Bristol Resurrection Men

This small graveyard belongs to the Church of St John the Baptist, also known as St John on the Wall. Though entry to the cemetery is rare, you can see through the fence to a peculiar, cube shaped stone building at the far end of the burial ground.

This was a cemetery lookout, an 18th century invention used to watch over the graves of freshly buried corpses. On the nights following a funeral, a watchman would be paid to look out over the cemetery to make sure none of the tombs were robbed by the loathed resurrection men - the nickname given to grave robbers.

This particular cemetery lookout was built sometime in the closing years of the 18th century and though it's not known if any resurrection men were ever successfully caught here, the need to build it is testament to the huge problem the city had with grave robbing.

In 1819 the church of St Augustine which used to stand on part of the ground which is now College Green, offered a huge and unprecedented reward of 50 guineas to anyone who caught a grave robber in the act. This reward seems not to have discouraged them as the churchyard continued to be targeted by resurrection men for many years afterwards. Incidentally, St Augustine Church was demolished in 1962 after falling into disrepair but it is believed that many of the cemetery corpses are still buried under College Green.

In South Bristol two resurrection men were caught in the middle of an attempt to haul the body of a freshly buried woman out of the ground in Hebron Road Cemetery. The two men narrowly avoided the gallows when it was revealed that they were doctors who needed corpses for dissection at the Bristol Royal Infirmary medical school.

The need for subjects for dissection seems to be the motive for the vast majority of grave robberies over the years, with large sums of money to be made by men who could withstand their morbid actions. The process wasn't curbed until the 1850s. It had been permitted to use the bodies of executed criminals for dissection a couple of decades before then, but it was only when laws were passed which allowed people to donate their bodies to medical science after death that the business of the resurrection men was finally stopped.

As gruesome as it may sound, grave robbers were filling a very vital role. At the time there was no means by which medical students could study dissection or anatomy aside from pictures and models or by attending autopsies. Though it may disturb modern sensibilities (as much as it did back then) it's also interesting to remember that without the resurrection men, the march of medical science would have been all but halted and we would likely be further behind in our medical knowledge today.

*Return to Broad Street and follow it uphill. Go across Corn Street and down the alleyway to the left of the Exchange Building until you come to a small church.*

## 7. The Grisly History of All Saint's Church

Depending on where you count the boundary of the city, and indeed, when you're doing it, All Saint's Church in St Nicholas Market may be the oldest church in Bristol.

Yes, there are older churches, most notably St James' Priory - generally thought of as the oldest building in Bristol but when this church was built the Priory was in a parish outside the boundary of the city. In the 12th century, the entirety of the city was what we now refer to as Old Town, the intersection of four streets, encircled by a protective wall.

What is undeniable is that this church has been at the heart of the city during some of its most harrowing times, the greatest of all being the bubonic plague.

The first outbreak hit the city in 1348 but for many years before that there had been word of a mysterious illness spreading across Europe, yet there was a general opinion that Britain, as an island, would remain safe. Of course it did not and the plague entered the country via one of its port cities (possibly Bristol itself).

In the first outbreak it spread almost instantaneously, killing at least half of the population of Bristol in a single year. At its peak it was said that the streets were so fearfully abandoned that long grass had grown throughout Bristol and that each morning, there would be a pile of bodies heaped up outside this church to be buried in plague pits outside of the city.

The plague returned in waves over several centuries and eventually left up to two thirds of the population dead. Although it's often suggested that the Great Fire of London finally put an end to the epidemic, medical historians now believe that it may have been due to the fact that the only people who remained alive in Europe were the descendants of those lucky enough to have had a genetic resistance to the disease - or to put it another way, the Great Plague had killed off everyone it possibly could.

The church was also the scene of one of the city's most enduring legends. During the reign of Henry VIII and his Dissolution of the Monasteries, soldiers loyal to the King and his newly founded Church of England were traveling around the city and forcefully converting Catholic buildings to Anglican ones, and in doing so, looting the religious buildings for whatever treasures could be found and executing any holy men who refused to convert.

When word reached All Saint's Church of what was happening across the country, the monks who operated here elected to strip the church of all of its valuables and to bury them in a secret location somewhere in the city. The rumours were true and the soldiers eventually came to Bristol and immediately captured the brother-hood of monks.

All the monks were executed and the secret location of their treasure, which would nowadays be worth a staggering fortune, died with them. It's astonishing to imagine that somewhere out there in our city there may be a hoard of priceless treasure which we are simply walking over every day.

*Come out of the alleyway where you will see the first of the bronze nails, a flat, circular-topped metal structure which will be our next point of interest.*

## 8. The Nails

One of Bristol's most famous oddities are its nails, four bronze, circular structures which stand at about chest height and are spaced out evenly before the beautiful Exchange Building, built in 1743.

They were originally placed in an alleyway on the opposite side of The Exchange to All Saint's Church and were underneath a waterproof fabric sheet to offer protection from the rain. The oldest, which is the furthest left when looking at The Exchange building, was cast sometime during the later years of the Elizabethan era while the newest dates back to 1631.

These served the purpose of offering a space for merchants and tradesmen to do business - and to do it in a manner that was out in the open - thus offering little opportunity for shenanigans to take place and also to suggest equity between the two merchants. The two men would place money or goods on the table (the ridged edges were to prevent coins from rolling away) and would exchange only when both were satisfied it was a fair deal.

Anyone who has heard of the nails will usually tell you that they are the source of the saying "cash on the nail" or "paying on the nail" to mean a speedy or immediate payment, and though it's possible that they were named after these nails, the same is also claimed by a handful of other cities which are also home to these structures. Although it's almost sacrilegious for me to say it, our sister city of Bath, which houses one in a covered market, is often considered to be the one the idiom was actually in reference to.

The area in front of the nails was also the scene of a very curious chapter in the history of Bristol. In 1899, Queen Victoria decided to pay the city a visit - her first in seventy years, and her arrival led to an enormous fanfare with an estimated 60,000 people lining the route her procession would take. When she came into Old Town, she entered in a horse-drawn carriage through the gate at the end of Broad Street and was met by cheers - cheers which quickly fell silent as people began to notice that the Queen had drawn the curtains to her carriage and was seated out of sight and in darkness. She was due to knight the city's first Lord Mayor Herbert Ashman outside the Exchange building but to the disappointed of all in attendance (and somewhat to the embarrassment of Ashman,) she invested, the Lord Mayor with a wave of her sword through the carriage window before returning to her seat and drawing the curtains once more.

No explanation was ever given for Queen Victoria's bizarre behaviour but it's been suggested that the frail 79 year old monarch, who'd grown increasingly displeased with large crowds, was simply in one of her "not amused" moods that cold, November day.

*You're pretty much at your next location already but get in a position where you have a good view of the Exchange Building clock.*

# 9. The Exchange Clock and Bristol Time

It doesn't take long to look at the handsome face of the Exchange Building clock before you realise something is slightly amiss.

The two minute hands, each ten minutes apart, may at first seem to defy logic but in fact tell a tale of an unusual chapter in British history and how we all once told the time.

Like all cities in Britain, Bristol had its own time. The difference between London and Penzance was about fifteen minutes, while Bristol lagged ten minutes behind what is now GMT or BST. This was due to the fact that towns and cities independently set their clocks by a sundial and the rise and fall of the sun determined a slight difference the further west one went.

For many centuries this was not an issue at all - travelling between cities could take a matter of days and a few extra minutes would have made no difference whatsoever, but with the advent of the train, particularly the Great Western Main Line in 1841, which could now transport people from Bristol to London in a matter of hours, people arrived at their final destination with their watches significantly different to local time.

Train timetables became a confusing mess of local times and many a journey was missed due to the esoteric nature of scheduling. Eventually a motion was put forward that the country should use a standardised time and that "Railway Time" - the measurement used by the railways in an attempt to avoid confusion - should be instigated nationwide.

Bristol being Bristol, a city which has never willfully bent to the whims of authority, decided instead that it would attempt to maintain its independent time zone and that Bristol Time would continue to operate for the locals, while an additional hand would be added to the Exchange Building to alert train passengers of Railway Time.

Bristol was not alone in this act of defiance, but we seem to have been the city most hell bent on sticking to it. As the city became more and more of a hub for nationwide railway travel this reticence began to seem more like bloody mindedness, so by 1853, Bristol finally fell in line with the rest of the country.

When I look at the second hand on the Exchange clock nowadays, I like to think of it as a reminder to all of us here that Bristol has always liked to do its own thing, and march just that little bit out of step with the rest of the country.

*Another tiny hop will take you to our final destination in Old Town, the end of Corn Street where it intersects with Broad Street, Wine Street and High Street.*

## 10. High Cross. Bristol's Elgin Marbles

The junction between Broad, Wine, High and Corn Streets was once home to one of our finest treasures, but unlike our other lost gems, this was not the fault of Luftwaffe bombers or thoughtless town planners, the blame for this loss lies with the casual indifference of certain people of the city.

High Cross was a market cross - a kind of marker used to denote where a town or city's market was held and was built to celebrate the 1373 charter by Edward III which made Bristol both a city and a county.

It was expanded in the 1630s, making it the largest non-church structure in Old Town, and as time passed, the likeness of monarchs were added to each of the four sides, to peer down each of the central roads of the city. Eventually there were eight figures; seven kings and a lone queen - Elizabeth I.

By the 1730s, Old Town was a bustling, metropolitan heart of what would (briefly) become the second largest city in the nation and soon complaints arose that the gargantuan, octagonal structure was getting in the way of the business of Bristol and that it had to be moved.

It was only when a local silversmith successfully lobbied that he feared for his life when high winds whipped around the spire of the monument that plans were put in place to move it.

After much negotiation as to where would be a suitable place for it (and a truly remarkable effort to move it,) by 1736 Bristol High Cross was standing in the middle of College Green.

By this time the Georgian era was underway and thanks to the waters of Hotwells the city was attracting visitors from across the country to partake in the fashionable exercise of bathing. With them came the endless display of "promenading" - the practice of wandering up and down the most illustrious areas of the city in ones finest outfits - in hopes of being seen and becoming the subject of envy (and gossip).

High Cross' placement had the undesirable effect of causing promenaders to have to break step in order to file past one by one and soon there were calls for the structure to be moved again (or even destroyed, as some people had argued.)

With barely a defender of the monument to be found among the city's elites, it was dismantled and placed in the care of the nearby cathedral for several decades until a new home was found for it - in the Stourhead Estate in Wiltshire, far away from Bristol.

During the Victorian era a group was founded in the hope of returning this ancient landmark to the city, but by this time it was seen as too fragile to risk moving it intact. An alternative plan was to rebuild the structure again within Bristol, but funds soon dried up when only the top section had been completed. The aborted attempt at a new High Cross can be found in Berkeley Square near Brandon Hill.

The battle to return High Cross to Bristol still continues (and the cross has been nicknamed "Bristol's Elgin Marbles") but the effort to do so would no doubt be a costly one. Unfortunately, due to short-sightedness and selfishness, this important relic from the ancient days of our city may now be lost forever.

*You have now reached the end of our tour of Old Town. If you wish to continue to a tour of Redcliffe and other nearby areas, follow High Street downhill until you reach Bristol Bridge.*

# Walk Two

## Redcliffe

# Redcliffe

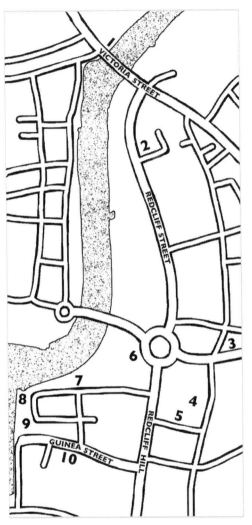

Our next journey through the hidden history of Bristol will take us through Redcliffe, one of the most fascinating, yet often overlooked corners of the city.

Though it's most famous for its breathtaking church, and its historic pubs, there's even more mystery and weirdness to be found right beneath your feet as you wander through this area.

Join me as we track down a tragic poet, a cat who had dozens attend his funeral and the most feared pirate of the seven seas.

# 1. The Brutal History of Bristol Bridge

Isambard Kingdom Brunel's masterpiece across the Avon Gorge may rightly be showered with praise and fame but sometimes it seems as if, in doing so, we forget that Bristol has another bridge which has been far more important to our history.

There has been a bridge crossing the River Avon at what is now Victoria Street since at least the 13th century - a bridge that was seen as such a technical marvel, as well as a vital route to and from what had been a closely knit web of hamlets, it offered our fledgling city its name "Brigstowe" - meaning "place by the bridge" in Old English.

The original bridge was very different to the one you see today. It was lined with five storey buildings on both sides, within which were homes, shops and even a small chapel. The buildings overhung the street so tightly that it was said people were able to shake hands with their neighbours through the upstairs windows, whilst at the rear, the overhang allowed toilets to empty directly into the river below.

The bridge was, however, a dark and dangerous place, with the land beyond it the haunt of highwaymen - the deadliest of whom were said to be able to bring down a horse with a single blade. The narrow street provided shadow and cover for criminals' nefarious deeds and by 1730 it was suggested that the bridge be scrapped and rebuilt anew, using funds that would be collected as tolls after the bridge was completed (tolls which they said would be removed once the bridge had met its construction costs.)

The new Bristol Bridge was completed in 1768 and is the one that can be seen today. Gone were the tall buildings and narrow walkways and now the bridge had clear sight-lines from either side. Its reputation as a dangerous hangout for criminals was over.

It took almost 25 years for the tolls to recoup the cost of the bridge's construction, but when it had been paid for in full, the city's mayor announced that not only would the tolls remain in place, but they would also be increased. More alarmingly, a row of nearby houses would be demolished to allow for expansion of a road.

The people reacted with immediate anger, gathering overnight in their hundreds along Bristol Bridge, at first to prevent any access across it in protest, and later to spread word of an overthrow of the local government.

With thoughts of the recent French Revolution in mind, the mayor saw fit to quickly dispel a potential radical uprising by sending in paid mercenaries to quash any rebellion, and the men went in with guns loaded.

It's not certain who pulled the trigger first or why it was pulled, but soon the protestors were in a hail of bullets. 11 people died on the first afternoon of the protest and a further 45 were seriously injured. It remains the bloodiest riot in Bristol's history and one of the most violent of 18th century Britain.

A potential rebellion may have been aborted at the expense of almost a dozen Bristolian lives, but the mayor of the city later claimed that the people of Bristol were prone to gathering in huge numbers at the first sign of injustice and that their obedience should not be taken for granted. The toll was later, quietly removed from Bristol Bridge.

*Cross the bridge with Old Town behind you and take a right turn onto Redcliff Street. Follow it for a short walk until you come to a narrow lane and the Seven Stars pub within it.*

## 2. The Abolitionists' Pub

The Seven Stars opened in 1694, making it among the handful of pubs to have survived intact from the 17th century. On the outside, you may notice a colourful plaque commemorating Thomas Clarkson - a man whose extraordinary legacy shines some light upon Bristol's often dark history.

Towards the end of the 1700s, Bristol's wealth and status as the second largest city in Britain had developed largely through international trade. Though many of Bristol's merchants believed themselves to have no involvement in the slave trade, those profiting from sugar, coffee and especially tobacco were, knowingly or not, deriving their money from the labour of slaves kept on plantations around the world - particularly America.

There were, of course, those who benefitted more directly from the trade in human beings, and Bristol was one of the first points of the "slave triangle" - with ships setting sail from the city to west Africa in order to imprison hundreds of slaves on tiny boats before forcing them into the hands of landowners in America in exchange for goods, which would then be brought back to Bristol.

This abhorrent trade remained largely hidden from many in Britain and race-based views held by much of the country saw African men, women and children as inferior to Europeans.

Thomas Clarkson, an abolitionist from Cambridgeshire, sought to challenge these racist opinions. When he came to Bristol in 1787, it was with the desire to expose the true horror of the abominable business and he soon found another sympathetic abolitionist in the form of the Seven Stars' landlord, who allowed Clarkson to set up an office in the establishment.

37

Over the course of several months, Clarkson began interviewing the sailors who came into the pub about the horrors they had witnessed whilst aboard slave ships. He catalogued these stories, along with examples of African art and crafts, in an effort to change perceptions of black people in the eyes of the British.

Clarkson took the ingenious step of not only presenting his document of stories from the Seven Stars to Parliament, but to also make it available to the general public. He knew that his pleas for the government to put an end to British involvement in the slave trade would likely fail in its first attempt, but he also believed that his document was persuasive - and harrowing enough to change public opinion.

He was right on both counts. The appeal was rejected by parliament but his document became widely read across the country, and just as he had hoped, pockets of resistance were founded and the general attitude towards the slave trade began to sour.

One person appalled by Clarkson's findings was a young William Wilberforce, the man who would go on to become the most famous abolitionist campaigner in British history, and whose tireless efforts to stop the trade in slaves would eventually see it outlawed in 1833.

Clarkson lived to see the British role in slavery ended and continued to lobby for an international ban until his death in 1846. Though he had longed to see the law changed far sooner, it cannot be denied that his attempts to alter public opinion were what first chipped away at an evil institution - and this humble little pub that had once been his office, became forever part of history.

*Continue back onto Redcliff Street and follow it to St Mary Redcliffe, take a left at the roundabout and go on a little until you see a sandstone stone facade of a building with a plaque reading "Thomas Chatterton, Poet".*

## 3. Bristol's Tragic Boy Poet.

There's something quite strange about the building on Redcliffe Way. A little east of St Mary Redcliffe Church is a squat stone building that seems to belong to a separate world to the modern office buildings and hotels which surround it on all sides. To look at it from the side it gets stranger still, as there's a completely different building behind it, wearing the front of another like a mask.

This frontage is all that remains of the school which educated Thomas Chatterton, Bristol's most famous - and most tragic - poet. The front of the building was all that was listed as a site of historic importance, and this is only due to the engraving over the door which gives the name of its most celebrated pupil.

Born in Bristol in 1752, Thomas Chatterton was a quiet, thoughtful boy who enjoyed his own company more than that of other children. As a voracious reader, he would lock himself away in the attic room of his house (a house which has since been demolished) to spend time with his books, but also to work on his other hobby.

By the age of eleven, Chatterton had, in secret, created a volume of poems which would become among the most celebrated of the Georgian era. However, due to his overwhelming shyness, the boy poet did not want the fame or recognition these works would no-doubt bring, so instead decided to bring them to the attention of the public in a manner which allowed him his anonymity.

He enlisted the help of Thomas Rowley, a long dead 15th century poet whose output had been stored in the library files of St Mary Redcliffe church. One day, whilst volunteering to catalogue the church's library, Chatterton claimed to have discovered Rowley's forgotten poems and introduced them to the Bristol literary elite.

They were an instant sensation. The exquisite romanticism of their words struck a chord with the people of the city, as did the curious story of their discovery. Chatterton's ruse did not last for long though, as he found it difficult to maintain his lie, and when he feared exposure (which did eventually happen) he fled to London where he hoped the confirmation of his talents would spur him on to make a living through his poetry.

However, it was not to be. Chatterton struggled to find inspiration and struggled even harder to make ends meet in his new city home. In 1770, aged only 17, he took his own life.

Chatterton never achieved the recognition he deserved in his lifetime, but probably would not have craved the inevitable fame that accompanied writers of his age. Sometime after his death, he was memorialised in oil paint by Henry Wallis in his startlingly dramatic "Death of Chatterton". Something about this morbid subject spoke to a new generation of Victorians who finally celebrated the boy-poet as among the finest of his time.

Although he's seldom read nowadays (classical romanticism has yet to undergo a revival in the poetry world) speculation does persist as to why the young man took his life. Some suggest it was because he was penniless, some say it was an accidental overdose of medicinal cyanide, but most agree that poor Thomas was just one of those tragic souls who simply feel things too much.

*Cross the road and journey on to St Mary Redcliffe. Near to the back (south side) entrance of the church there is a small headstone embedded in the grass reading "The Church Cat".*

## 4. Tom the Church Cat

St Mary Redcliffe is, without a doubt, the grandest church in Bristol. It is a monument to medieval ingenuity and religious faith, and a church which most Bristolians will tell you was described by Queen Elizabeth I on her 1574 visit to Bristol as the "fairest, goodliest and most famous parish church in England."

Only she almost certainly didn't say this. The earliest record of the quote appears to come from nearly fifty years after her visit to Bristol and her itinerary seems not to have even brought her close to this part of the city. However, had she said such a thing, few people would have argued, as this magnificent church is something to behold.

Heavily ornamented with curious creatures and stylised depictions of saints, the church can boast almost thirty appearances of "The Green Man" - an enigmatic Pagan figure of which little is known, but whose likeness adorned many early churches as a means of marrying together Britains old and new religions. It also features some extraordinary human likenesses that are thought to be caricatures of church workers and congregation members from the 16th century.

They churchyard of St Mary Redcliffe is notably sparse when it comes to headstones, but one of note can be found hidden away in the grass near the church's south entrance.

Just visible through almost a hundred years of lichen growth are the words *"THE CHURCH CAT 1912-1927"* and as you may expect, this is exactly who is buried here.

The story of Tom, the black and white cat who was so beloved by his adopted church began on a stormy night, when a hungry cat came scratching at the church door. The reverend at the time took pity on the soaking feline and invited him inside, whereupon he immediately found a pew to sleep on until the storm had subsided.

Only he didn't leave. He kept on returning, and soon the congregation were leaving him food and treats and he, in exchange, ensured that the massive church was free of rats and mice. In no time the cat had taken up near full-time residence in the church (although, at least one family nearby was also his casual acquaintance) and was often seen sleeping or cleaning himself near the altar during services.

So loved was Tom by the congregation, that when he died aged around 15 years old, he was given a full church funeral which was attended by dozens of locals wishing to bid him a final farewell.

He was buried in the ground in a handmade coffin, a little under a foot in length, just in front of the door where he had once, fifteen years before, asked for help on a wet and stormy night.

*Stay in St Mary Redcliffe churchyard for our next location - the piece of metal jutting out of the ground towards the iron railing along the Colston Parade side.*

## 5. The St Mary Redcliffe Tram Rail

The churchyard of St Mary Redcliffe holds one of the strangest artifacts from WWII - an unmistakably out of place piece of metal jutting incongruously from the ground at an impossible angle.

It may be hard to imagine but this is a section of iron tramway, once buried in the road two streets away. An enormous bomb tore it from the ground and sent it soaring high over the row of houses along Colston Parade, where it pierced the ground of the churchyard and has remained ever since.

Before the war, Bristol was crisscrossed with tram lines, the earliest of which opened in 1875 and trams were pulled along by horses. The first electric tram was introduced to the city in 1895 and eventually there were 17 different routes laid out in tramways all across Bristol.

Many of the tramways were destroyed during the Bristol Blitz but it was the rise of the city bus as a cheap and dependable means of travel which eventually made the trams obsolete.

Most of the bombs which fell on Bristol during the six major Luftwaffe raids were incendiary bombs, which destroyed through heat and near inextinguishable fires, so the bomb which propelled the tram track into the ground was a somewhat unusual one. Incendiary bombs were dropped because a great deal of Bristol was, at the time, made of wood. The Luftwaffe needed only to start the fire which would soon turn into an unstoppable inferno.

These incendiary bombs had been responsible for melting the roof of St Philip's Church on what is now Castle Park and there had been such worry that Bristol would lose all its churches if the blitz continued that volunteers spent their nights in many of the city's most prominent and ancient churches.

At St Mary Redcliffe, about a dozen men (often among them was the church's vicar) camped out on the roof. It had been observed that incendiary bombs blazed only slightly on first reaching their target, which meant that speedy guardians of the church roof could kick away these devices before they burst into flames - which is precisely what they did, undoubtedly saving our grandest church many times over.

The section of tramway in the grass is kept not just as a memorial to the lives that were lost in the surrounding area, but also as a reminder of just how close the city's finest church came to total destruction.

*We're now leaving St Mary Redcliffe and going in search of the Quaker Burial Ground, which is the small park tucked away on the opposite side of Redcliff Hill.*

## 6. The Quaker Burial Ground

Bristol has had a long association with the Quakers, with many of our most notable merchants and families being among the Society of Friends - especially those connected with the trade in chocolate and tobacco. It's also worth remembering that while many of the 18th century Quaker families profited greatly from the slave trade, the Quakers were among the first in the country to eventually condemn the practice and to lobby for it being outlawed.

This small park used to be considerably bigger and was once a burial ground for Quakers. Established in 1665 it is among the oldest in the city.

More ancient still is the cave to be found at the back of the burial ground. This man-made alcove was cut into the soft sandstone rock in 1346 (its red colour and the sheer edifice is what gives Redcliffe its name). It was a hermitage, built to house a hermit - a devoutly religious person who could be employed to pray for wealthy families.

The first hermit to live here was John Sparkes, and though little is known of him, he was in the employ of Thomas Lord Berkeley for some years, and after his departure, a succession of hermits replaced him over the course of many centuries until it was eventually taken over by the Quakers.

By the 1960s, plans to rebuild the war-ravaged city were finally in full effect and the only obstacle to what was to be a ring road encircling and occasionally crossing the city was the Quakers Burial Ground, which had been out of use since 1923 - due to Quakers by then favouring cremation as a means of body disposal.

Among Quaker societies in the city there was a general mood that hanging on to this bit of land was rather ostentatious for a group noted for its generosity, so in 1969 it was officially gifted by them to the city council and work began at once on what was to become one of the most hated and historically destructive planning decisions ever made by the city - the roundabout in front of St Mary Redcliffe.

One of the more bizarre relics from this period can be found in the hermitage. If you peer through the metal bars that now prevent access to the cave you will see piles and piles of flat stones stacked upon one another - these are the headstones of the Quakers who were buried here over the centuries, left as a somewhat forgotten shambles in the corner of the park.

So where did the bodies go? As morbid as it may be to think about, they're all still down there. The headstones were removed but the graves were built on. Beneath your feet in the park or beneath your tyres as you drive around the roundabout are the remains of hundreds, if not thousands of human bodies.

*With that delightful thought in our heads, it's time to leave the Quaker Burial Ground. With your back to St Mary Redcliffe church, head towards the Floating Harbour and take a left turn through the wall before you reach the water. Follow the harbour until you reach a ramp in the red cliff and look for a metal gate through which you can see an underground tunnel.*

## 7. The Redcliffe Caves

Peering through the metal gates which seal off the Redcliffe Caves from the public, it's near impossible to look into the darkness and get any real sense of just what an important and fascinating piece of Bristol history is woven through the red sandstone cliffs.

If you've ever seen a map of the various underground tunnels and waterways that zigzag under our city, it's easy to imagine the Bristol beneath our feet as something akin to Swiss cheese, and this is no more apparent than with the Redcliffe Caves.

Although they're almost always referred to as caves, they're entirely man-made and should therefore be more properly referred to as mines.

Beginning in the latter stages of the Middle Ages, it had been discovered that the sand on which Redcliffe stood was of the exact granulation best suited for manufacturing glass and porcelain and over the course of many centuries this sand was hollowed out of the cliffs, reaching a peak around about the 18th century when international demand for glassware made it a highly valuable commodity.

As with so many aspects of Bristol's history of international trade, this glassware played a major role in the enslavement of Africans who were sold in exchange for the glass and then taken to plantations in America.

Rumours persist that slaves were forced to live in the Redcliffe Caves, with stories of them being chained to the walls when not being put to work. Mercifully, these stories seem to be untrue. There is some evidence that during the Napoleonic Wars, French prisoners were kept in the caves and likely were chained to the walls, so this may be the origin of the story.

During the Second World War, the caves were repurposed for the people of Redcliffe as shelters which could be used in the event of an air raid. It's believed that several families made use of them during this period and in at least one instance, had a very fortunate escape.

On the same night that an explosive sent a tram rail flying into the grounds of St Mary Redcliffe church, another massive bomb landed above a section of the caves. Upon detonating, it permanently sealed off a large section of mostly uncharted caves which was believed to stretch for miles of labyrinthine tunnels across the region. For this reason, it's a mystery as to just how long the Redcliffe Caves system actually is.

If you're interested in seeing more evidence of the city's history of glassmaking, I recommend a stroll over to nearby Prewett Street where the last remaining kiln to survive in Bristol is currently been used as a restaurant. Its unusual, flat-topped conical shape is unmistakable. It would have once towered over the area, billowing smoke as it smelted sand and would have been one of a dozen closely packed around the Redcliffe area.

*Keep following the harbour towards The Ostrich pub, but before you get there, look for a concrete slope running down to meet the water. Across the harbour you should be able to see the Riverstation.*

## 8. The Forgotten River Crossing

At first glance, the concrete ramp going down to meet the water from the Ostrich pub garden seems to be nothing out of the ordinary, after all, there are plenty of similar ramps to be found all around the harbour, but on closer inspection, there's more to this spot than first meets the eye.

Though it certainly has been used to launch boats for many years, its original purpose was a rather ingenious solution to what had been Bristol's most abiding problem - the rise and fall of the river.

If you stand beside the water's edge at the bottom of this ramp, you may catch a glimpse of cobbled stones beneath the surface. If the conditions are particularly favourable, you may even be lucky enough to spy the impression of a ridge running through the harbour. This may be the city's first ever river crossing.

Running along what was then a river bed and emerging at the opposite side (now used as a place to store small boats beneath the Riverstation where a similar ramp emerges), this man-made ridge allowed people to cross from one side of the river to the other at low tide.

Before the creation of the Floating Harbour, which ensured the docks were perpetually full, Bristol was at the mercy of the relentless tide. Aside from it causing problems for vessels coming in and out, it essentially separated the people of Redcliffe and Bedminster from Bristol when the river was high. This was no small problem for the mainly rural inhabitants of those areas, who would struggle to get to market to sell their goods. This wasn't an issue if you were selling bags of grain as you could get a boat across the water, but successfully transporting a cow into Bristol this way was never going to work.

The solution was the river crossing. Using this ridge across the Avon, tradespeople now had a wider window in which to reach the city as even at a medium tide there was a chance you could wade across the stone footpath, and it was sturdy enough to drive cattle over too.

The history of this crossing is somewhat murky but it's been suggested it may have been built in the early 13th century, meaning it would have pre-dated Bristol Bridge by several decades and if true, would make it the first permanent structure built to help people cross the river.

*You're virtually there. Our next stop is The Ostrich. There's plenty to see from the outside but I recommend popping in to see a section of the Redcliffe Caves.*

## 9. The Ostrich

If you come to the Ostrich on a hot, summer's evening, you'll see why it's one of Bristol's most popular pubs, with its enormous seating area often filled to overflowing on weekends, but its popularity is nothing new, in fact, its location has acted like a magnet for many different people over the centuries.

It opened around 1745 and was an immediate hit with sailors and international merchants. At that time you would likely see people from all over the world who were stationed in the city, sometimes for weeks at a time.

These were the days when pubs regularly scattered sawdust over their floors, to make the job of cleaning up spilled beer, vomit and occasionally blood considerably easier at the end of the night.

However, it's believed that the Ostrich favoured using sand from the nearby caves as a free and readily available alternative. A handful of boys were employed each day to crawl into the tunnels and return with sand. These boys were likely paid a small amount of money and almost certainly beer. Nicknamed "sandboys" their drunken, merry demeanours are said to have coined the phrase "as happy as a sandboy". Could this be true? It's certainly possible. Phrase origins are notoriously difficult to track down but the evidence for the Ostrich having birthed this saying seems entirely plausible.

The sailors and seafarers who frequented the Ostrich had reason to need a layer of sand beneath their feet. Often locked away for weeks at a time in vessels, a visit to the port of Bristol was a rare opportunity for some cider-fuelled debauchery. If the timing was favourable to ships coming into the harbour, a crew of seamen could find themselves in Bristol for several days at a time until conditions to leave were right.

The perilous rise and fall of the Avon made navigating its waters no mean feat as a single mistake by an impatient captain who didn't want to wait for an appropriate tide could break a ship in an instant.

Even when the tides were suitable, it was important to perfectly balance a vessel that was to be docked in the harbour. A poorly maintained ship could easily topple over on the rocky riverbed of the Avon. The urgency to strictly manage the contents of a ship coming into the city gave rise to the phrase "ship shape and Bristol fashion".

For captains who were especially concerned for their ship's safety, there was one other alternative. A small section of the river did not have a rocky bed beneath it, but a soft mound of silt on which a ship could safely rest at low tide, cushioned enough that it probably would not capsize. This area was, and continues to be known as, the Mud Dock.

One other curiosity for which the Ostrich is known can be found inside. A section of wall has been knocked through, into which you can see quite a lengthy section of the Redcliffe Caves. Don't be too alarmed by the skeleton, it's a replica!

*From here we're heading to another pub, this time the Golden Guinea, which is a short walk from the Ostrich. Join Guinea Street, adjacent to the Ostrich pub garden and follow it up the hill.*

## 10. Blackbeard the Pirate

It may be hard to believe but Guinea Street, the charming, quiet street that runs through Redcliffe, was likely the birthplace of the most feared pirate of the seven seas.

Born somewhere along the street around about 1680, Edward Teach (or Thatch) would go on to become the world's most famous pirate - Blackbeard.

If it sounds as if the known facts are shaky, it's because they are. Records from the era are somewhat patchy and though it's not 100% certain that Teach was born on this street (or indeed that he was even a Bristolian) most historians agree that the evidence points to Guinea Street as the place where he was born.

Number 10, Guinea Street is often suggested as a possible candidate for the birthplace of the man who would become Blackbeard, but this seems to be little more than local legend owing to an unusual carving of a bearded man's head, rumoured to be Teach. While the house is possibly old enough to have been standing in 1680, the street would've been lined with similar homes at the time and the bearded face is most likely just a generic depiction of a man.

Whoever Edward Teach was, he seems to have spent his early years in the city as a relatively law abiding young man. He is believed to have frequented a number of pubs in the area, but locals would later claim that the Golden Guinea was his most regular haunt. It may well have been here that Edward Teach first met sailors and later sought work with them, leaving Bristol aged about 20 in the company of privateers.

What happened to Edward Teach over the following years is a mystery, but the sea certainly seems to have had a corrupting effect on the man because he emerges again in 1716, now a fully fledged pirate going by the name of Blackbeard and in command of a French ship he had captured and renamed The Queen Anne's Revenge.

Blackbeard was one of those rare people about whom legends are created while they're still alive. Tales that he was stronger than an ox and that he had a beard made out of pure fire (a rumour likely propagated by Blackbeard himself, who is said to have hidden burning matches in his beard to appear more frightening). Most alarmingly, it was said that the pirate had a heart as merciless as the sea itself, which was enough to strike fear into sailors the world over.

In truth there are no records of Blackbeard ever having killed or mistreated those he had captured and accounts suggest he ran quite a fair and democratic ship with a crew of sailors who were well paid and onboard voluntarily. Blackbeard's masterstroke seems to have been one of marketing. If you make yourself the most feared man on the sea, there is no need to even engage in battle as your opponents would rather surrender than fight you.

Blackbeard couldn't avoid every conflict though, and he was killed in battle in 1718, where it was claimed that the headless pirate's body swam thirteen times around his ship before dying.

Edward Teach had command of the oceans for only two short years, but his legend would go on forever.

*To continue on to the next walk through south Bristol, follow Guinea Street to Redcliff Hill and take a right turn. Your first stop will be Bedminster Bridge, where it crosses the New Cut.*

# Walk Three
## South Of The River

## South of the River

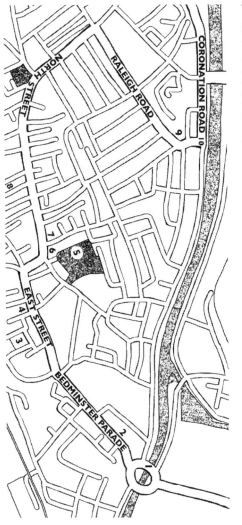

Though they may be less of a tourist draw than some of Bristol's more prestigious neighbourhoods, the twin areas of Bedminster and Southville have enjoyed a proud history of their own.

For much of its existence, the residential areas south of the river have not been part of Bristol at all, and as such, have stories to tell that are unique and completely separate from the rest of the city.

Join me on a tour of south Bristol, where we'll encounter a mysterious princess with a secret, a man-eating lion and a brood of ferocious, feral chickens...

# 1. Carving the New Cut

It may not look at first to be anything beyond a deep river, but the Bristol New Cut is without a doubt, the most vital waterway in the whole city, as without it the Floating Harbour and Bristol as we now know it could not exist.

The Floating Harbour is so named as it was built to ensure that water was maintained at the level of high tide continuously within Bristol. This meant that boats could remain floating in the city, regardless of the ebb and flow of the River Avon. But all that water rushing towards the city had to go *somewhere* - which is why the New Cut is so very important.

It's astonishing to imagine, but the entirety of the almost two mile river diversion that runs from Cumberland Basin to Netham Weir was carved out by human labour.

This jaw-dropping feat required an enormous task force of hundreds of navvies - navigational engineers who worked on large-scale engineering projects across the world. Although an oft-repeated rumour would have you know that French prisoners of the Napoleonic Wars were forced into work alongside them, there's no real evidence of this.

The navvies were a mixture of English and Irish men who took five years to pickaxe and shovel their way through the earth, with explosives utilised whenever they struck upon enormous rocks.

From the start of construction in 1804, tensions were high between the Irish and English workers, with fights breaking out regularly between the two sides. It's unclear what was the cause of this friction, but it's likely to have been nothing more than old-fashioned nationalism.

The final stage of constructing the waterway was to use dynamite to blow apart the front and back end of the New Cut, allowing water from the Avon to flow freely through the newly built diversion, at which point, the locks leading into Bristol harbour were sealed, and the city would never again be at the mercy of the destructive tides.

The engineering marvel was the toast of Bristol, indeed, the entire country. Never before had such a large scale project been completed in such a short space of time (a little under five years.)

To celebrate this achievement, an enormous banquet was held for the hard working navvies, and over a thousand of them were invited to attend. It was hosted on Spike Island in the open air on a fine May afternoon, and each of those in attendance was was permitted an abundance of meat and potatoes - and a gallon of strong beer - which is a little under eight pints.

The celebrations began jovially enough, with the English and Irish seemingly happy to put aside their differences to join in a mutual celebration, but as the festivities drew into the night and as the alcohol began to dry up, fights started breaking out between the workers, at first small scale but rapidly escalating until the entire banquet had turned into a brawl.

The scene of drunken violence was so alarming, that officials had to act fast, rounding up press gangs who usually spent their time coaxing (or forcing) people to work on ships and sending them to Spike Island to break up what had become a full-scale riot.

A night of violence aside, we have much to thank the navvies for. Without the incredible New Cut, Bristol would not be the Bristol we know today.

*The next stop will take us to the Old Police Station, the castle-like building on Bedminster Parade. Cross the bridge and follow Bedminster Parade until you get to the grey building a couple of doors down from the Bedminster Library.*

## 2. The Old Police Station

The Old Police Station on Bedminster Parade is an immediately arresting building. It once would have towered above the area but now stands out simply as an unusual design in an innocuous place. Even if you know nothing of this building's history, something about it just seems suggest it has an unusual story to tell.

By the 1880s, Bedminster had gone through something of a population explosion. Coal being discovered in the area brought wave after wave of workers to the suburb in search of employment but the streets were all but deserted at night.

There was only one streetlamp in all of Bedminster, and East Street and Bedminster Parade were notorious for their late night muggings (pickpockets, whose nimble fingers needed daylight, operated during the day) but the nearest police station was to be found miles away.

Even more perilous were the fires. Many houses were still lit primarily with candles with night and with families crammed into small rooms, accidents were inevitable. Something had to be done.

The police station on Bedminster Parade was the last of Bristol's police stations to be built during the Victorian era, and the last of three to have been funded with an 1850 endowment from Parliament.

It opened in 1883, having been built to a design planned over a decade before. The reason for the delay seems to have been a rather unsympathetic one - the areas of the city where wealthier people lived, had access to police far more readily - it also explains why it was one of the final buildings to be built, or at least inspired by the Bristol Byzantine architectural style (more info on that can be found on the seventh walk in this book).

The effect of the police station in the area seems to have been instantaneous. Criminal gangs would now have to operating under the noses of the police at night so they were forced elsewhere (or to seek more law-abiding careers) and the knock on effect of safer streets meant that more pubs opened around Bedminster.

Perhaps the most significant change to the lives of residents in the area can be found atop the police station. The peculiar turret protruding from its roof is actually a lookout. The station was also home to a handful of firemen who worked in shifts on this tower, keeping a watchful eye over south Bristol for signs of fire.

In the past, fire brigades had operated on an insurance basis. Working as private firms, they would attend houses that were ablaze but only put them out if the house displayed a metal badge on its exterior, proving that the homeowners had paid their insurance dues (an example of one of these fire-badges still exists on the Tudor cottages at the bottom of Christmas Steps). Otherwise the house would be left or to burn, or the residents would have to hastily barter a payment to the fire fighters at the scene of the blaze.

A curious feature of this law meant that if your neighbour was insured, so likely were you, as a fire which started in your home would have to be extinguished for fear of it spreading to the insured home next door.

In one of the poorest areas of Bristol, like Bedminster, very few people would have had the money to afford the insurance payments. Though, at this time, there had been fire brigades across Bristol which operated on local government money and private donations, this was the first which was built to explicitly serve the people of south Bristol, and likely saved countless lives in its years of operation.

This simple building may not look like much, but it improved the lives for countless people in the area and was one of the first true advances in improving the living conditions of the working poor of Bristol.

*Stay on Bedminster Parade until it reaches East Street. When you see Church Road on the left, follow this uphill until you come to a small park.*

## 3. The Lost Church and Bedminster's Blitz

It's a matter of pride among the people of Bedminster, that the area south of the river has been established longer than Bristol itself.

In fact, when the first few hamlets were being built on the grassland of what is now Old Town, Bedminster was already a somewhat populous village with its own church and market.

One of the first churches to be built in the area once towered over where St John's Park now stands. This tranquil little park was formerly the grounds of a religious building, which was established in 1003.

Over the centuries the church experienced a tumultuous life, including being ransacked by Henry VIII's soldiers and then being burnt to the ground in 1645 during the Civil War, but it was rebuilt, twice in fact, and by the mid 18th century it was known as the Church of St John the Baptist, and it was the primary church for most of Bedminster. It's believed that parts of it may have even dated back to the original 1003 structure.

But with the advent of World War II came bombs, and on the night of the 24th of November, two incendiary bombs singed through the roof and gutted the building within hours.

It remained standing as a burnt out skeleton for 27 years until it was finally torn down, but in the park you can find a rather curious looking lump of stone which, upon closer inspection, reveals itself to be a kind of animal figure, draped in carefully chiselled ivy. It's unclear what this figure was supposed to represent but it was once housed in the church and kept somewhere near the altar.

Bedminster was of absolutely no strategic importance to Nazi Germany but it was bombed extensively during the Bristol Blitz. It may have been targeted because it was mistakenly identified as the docks or, more likely, it was the victim of pure bad luck and happened to lay near the Luftwaffe's intended targets. After completing their missions the pilots probably simply lightened the weight of their aircraft by jettisoning their arsenal onto south Bristol before returning home.

Bedminster may have been ill-fated in its positioning, but it was also subject of extraordinary good luck.) On the same night that St John's Church was lost, an enormous bomb, nicknamed "The Satan Bomb" was dropped onto Bedminster a few streets away from the church. It embedded itself into the ground but mercifully did not detonate - for if it had, the nine foot long explosive would have turned much of the surrounding streets into a crater and taken hundreds, if not thousands of lives in an instant.

*Return to East Street and take a left turn. There is a small alleyway between 143 and 145 East Street. Go through here until you find a set of stone steps.*

## 4. The Bedminster Crapper

Weird history can be found everywhere in Bristol, but down an alleyway which is squeezed between a hair salon and a casino may not be the first place you'd choose to start looking for it. However, this narrow passage behind the world-famous Cameron Balloons is home to one of the earliest inventions of a man who would become a legend of his time.

At the bottom of these steps is a manhole cover, it is finely decorated with concentric circles as well as the name of its designer - "Crapper" - Thomas Crapper, the sanitation expert who literally helped the Victorian era be flushed with success.

This manhole cover is likely from the early 1860s when Crapper had purchased a brass foundry in London to build his designs.

Though he's often credited with inventing the flush toilet and also the toilet S-bend, neither of these patents belonged to him. Crapper was a pioneer in his age, mostly for changing the way in which people spoke about lavatories. He invited the notoriously prudish Victorians to visit showrooms where he exhibited flush toilets alongside other bathroom and plumbing fittings and in doing so, made the toilet a suitable topic of conversation.

During the period when this manhole cover was installed, Bedminster could boast only a single flushing toilet and the construction of the Bristol New Cut had made the area considerably more unsanitary. Before it was built, most of the city had emptied their chamber pots into drains which washed into Avon, but with the creation of the Floating Harbour, it became an offense to do so - as the "waste matter" would simply bob around the harbour without tides to carry it away.

Drains were instead rerouted to the New Cut, meaning that twice a day, as the tidal direction changed, there was a good hour or so in which an entire city's effluence was drifting over south Bristol.

Worse still, when the Malago River flooded (as it often did before improved drainage in the 1960s) the river itself could backup, bringing with it unwanted gifts that would end up bobbing through the streets.

Crapper's manhole cover, and the drain which lay beneath it, did not do much to improve these conditions immediately, but with time, his improvements to how cities dealt with the things they'd rather not talk about, made gradual steps in bettering the sanitary conditions with which we all must live.

*Return once more to East Street and continue along to a backstreet named Dean Street. Follow it to the end and take a right onto Dean Lane. Our destination is Dame Emily Park and the hexagonal slab of concrete that is jutting out of the ground near the skate park.*

## 5. Dame Emily Park

Towards the skate park area of this lovely green space along Dean Lane is an inconspicuous slab of concrete jutting out of the ground, with steps going up to it.

Not that long ago, this was the park's bandstand but a little before then, it was the open mouth of one of the largest mine shafts in south Bristol.

Coal mining began in Bedminster during the 1670s. At that time, coal could only be mined at the surface with pickaxes, and though it was theorized that a deeper seem could be running beneath what was then mostly farmland, the technology did not exist to access it.

In 1748, experiments with dynamite were held to attempt to blast through the top rock to the coal beneath and when these proved successful, mine shafts began opening across the region.

It was during this period that Bedminster experienced its largest ever population explosion. Over the next 150 years, the number of people living in Bedminster swelled from about 3,000 to over 70,000.

It was hard work, but it was dependable and required unskilled labour, so it attracted workers from across the country, and to accommodate this population boom, streets of terraced houses were built all across the south Bristol. Many of these streets were even named in after precious stones, in honour of mining as an industry - Beryl Street, Garnet Road, Ruby Street and Jasper Street.

Of course, it was no not precious stones that the men of Bedminster were mining, but coal, and it was extremely dangerous. Aside from the ever present danger of breathing in coal dust, the miners were at risk from rock falls, poisonous gas and even drowning if pickaxes accidentally struck through the mine wall to an underground waterway. About one man every month died in the south Bristol mines.

The seam beneath Bedminster was part of a complex system of coal fields which stretched across north Somerset, rising close to the surface in several points across the county, but nowhere was it found in such abundance as it was south of the River Avon. The mine owners had every reason to suspect that the coal would never run out, but that's exactly what happened.

The coal pit beneath what is now Dame Emily Park was mined hollow by 1906 and it was established that all of the coal had simply been brought out of the ground. The same fate soon befell the remaining mines and by the 1940s, the very last of them was closed forever.

*Return to Dean Lane for a very short walk. Follow it to North Street and the first pub you will come across is the highly decorated Steam Crane. This will be our next stop on the tour.*

## 6. A Gruesome Night at the Bull.

The steam Crane pub has had quite a notorious history, including being the scene of the trial of John Horwood - the 19th century murderer whose trial caused a national sensation and whose skin was later used to bind his own trial notes.

However, it is for a single night in 1827 for which the pub is most infamous, and an incident that shocked all of the city.

Pubs along North Street had been cashing in on the influx of new residents to Bedminster over the intervening decades and the street had yet to fall victim to the crimewave East Street was experiencing. Drinking establishments were in direct competition with one another, and drinks were already at rock bottom prices to accommodate the miners' slender wages. In order to draw in the crowds, the landlord of this Steam Crane (then named the Bull) came up with an idea - a gimmick.

Mr Martin attended a travelling menagerie on Bristol harbour one night and saw how much the exotic animals were entertaining the crowds. Travelling menageries were a sort of forerunner to both the modern circus and zoos. They travelled around the country exhibiting animals from around the world in cages, to the delight and sometimes terror of onlookers.

Mr Martin was clearly an impulsive man and decided on the spot to buy one of the exhibition's lions. It's unknown how much this set him back but it must have been quite a fortune. Soon his pub had a remarkable new attraction - a fully grown lion, which was kept in a metal cage at the side of the bar.

As expected, this was an immediate hit with the people of Bristol, who travelled across the city to visit this curious and incredible animal. For many of the pub's new clientele, this would have been their first encounter with a lion.

Perhaps this naivety goes some way to explain the horrors of that night. A little while after the lion was brought to the Bull, the rowdy and no doubt inebriated patrons of the bar were growing weary of the lion's lazy attitude when it came to entertaining them.

Lion's can sleep for up to twenty hours a day and care little for keeping time with humans' schedules. The crowd demanded entertainment and Mr Martin came up with a plan on the spot.

He offered the barman, Joseph Kiddle, some extra money at the end of the night if he got in the cage with the animal. Kiddle was reluctant, but this extra money was likely quite a sum, so he was eventually persuaded to enter the lion's den.

At first, the lion did not seem to respond or even stir much and eventually it was decided that Kiddle should attempt pulling a pint through the bars of the cage. It seems to be during this process that the lion attacked.

Poor Joseph Kiddle was not only killed, but torn to shreds and eaten in front of a pub full of horrified on-lookers.

Quite astonishingly, the lion remained on display the following night, only now his fur was flecked with the blood of the young man - unsurprisingly this proved even more of a draw for the punters, who now could witness not just a lion, but a bona fide man-eater too. The pub's popularity was secured, as was its part in the gruesome and truly weird history of Bristol.

*Our next stop is just a few doors up. Follow North street to the corner with Merrywood Road, where a carving that reads "Poet's Corner" can be seen on the second floor of a building.*

## 7. The Butcher Poet

Above an estate agent at the east end of North Street, a weathered and somewhat neglected bust of a man surveys the street below. It's the kind of peculiar street decoration you could walk past a hundred times without ever really noticing it, but once you've heard the charming story behind the man who inspired it, it's hard to forget.

Bedminster has had its fair share of eccentrics over the years, but few are as fondly remembered as the butcher/poet Alfred Dawes Collard.

Born into a family which had been the proprietors of butcher shops across south Bristol since at least the 1770s, Alfred was destined for a life in meat and though he seemed happy fulfilling his destiny, he also craved a more creative outlet.

Opening his own butchers on North Street - which can still be seen today across the street at the corner of Braunton Road (the shop still has the original tiling around its base which features Alfred's name) his literary aspirations took the form of poetry, most notably, his peculiar penchant for rhyming couplets on the theme of meat, including one which name checked every butcher shop in Bristol.

Meat-based poetry was always going to be a minority interest in the literary world, but his works took on an unusual life of their own when they began to be read around the city, and soon Alfred had a handful of fans, eager to read his latest creations.

Were these fans mocking Alfred's works? Probably. It wasn't just their bizarre subject matter which raised eyebrows but also his clumsy rhyme schemes. He was once described as "a butcher of both meats and of the English language."

Alfred seems to have been completely unfazed by his notoriety and may even have enjoyed being celebrated as "the worst poet in Bristol" because he later self-published a folio of his collected works and donated all of the profits to the local hospital.

He died sometime around 1882, about the time that "Poet's Corner" was established on North Street. There are two theories as to what this unusual monument was actually in honour of.

The first is that Alfred Dawes Collard financed it himself, not to celebrate his own works but those of his favourite poets, Coleridge and Wordsworth, both of whom had first found success in Bristol, where a printing works was the first to publish their poetry.

The second, which is the more commonly believed, is that it was built as a memorial to Alfred himself, and that money was raised by the people of Bedminster, so that a permanent dedication to the butcher poet would forever look over the street he had once called his home.

*From one dreamer to another, we are going in search of one more local hero who defied all expectations of class and status. Stay on North Street and follow it to Melville Terrace. Go up the hill until you reach the small cemetery.*

## 8. The Lost Grave of Princess Caraboo

Somewhere in an unmarked plot in Hebron Road Cemetery are the remains of the woman the world would know as Princess Caraboo, the most beloved fraudster in Bristol history.

The story of the mysterious princess began in 1817 when a woman was found wandering the marshes of Almondsbury in Gloucestershire. She was dressed in a fine gown which was spattered with mud and wore an ornate head dress, the likes of which the people of the small town had never seen before.

The woman seemed startled, and although she spoke no English, it was clear that she was in some distress. Eventually she was taken to the town's magistrate who, both concerned for her welfare and intrigued by this strange woman, allowed her to stay at his family's home on the Knowle Estate.

She adjusted to the high life very quickly, favouring exotic fruits to meat and enjoying fine wine. Though she had yet to speak a single word, people travelled from all over the region to visit this enchanting woman.

She was proficient at archery and demonstrated a keen ability at painting, but some of her more eccentric habits must have caused some concern among the people of Gloucestershire, not least her penchant for bathing nude in the local river.

With some patience and the use of illustrations, as well as a translator from Bristol who claimed to be able to understand the woman's native tongue, it was established that she was no ordinary woman, but a princess.

Her story was that she was Princess Caraboo, the heir to the throne of the kingdom of Javascu, an island nation in the Indian Ocean. Whilst travelling to Britain on a ship, the vessel was boarded by pirates and she was forced to dive overboard into the Bristol Channel where she swam with the tide until she washed ashore at the Almondsbury marshes.

This extraordinary tale astonished all of Gloucestershire and soon she was dining each evening with dukes and duchesses and reporters were visiting her every morning to share her remarkable story.

This proved to be Princess Caraboo's downfall, as one of these reporters included a reproduction of an illustration of her. Immediately a letter was sent by a Bristol woman, informing the household that the woman was no Princess, but Mary Baker, a Bedminster leech seller.

The gig was up and Mary confessed to the story. She had been little more than a beggar woman in the streets of Bristol and Gloucestershire for many years, making ends meet by selling leeches to apothecaries whenever she could. The idea to escape the drudgery of her life had been a hasty one after a wealthy woman had gifted her a dazzling gown. The head dress she had stitched herself.

She had not intended for things to go as far as they did and had only hoped for a room for a night or two, but once she was the subject of aristocratic intrigue, she decided she would go along with this new life, wherever it took her.

It would be easy to imagine that the household would react to this revelation with anger, but surprisingly, she was not only forgiven for her deceit, but the family (who had clearly been as charmed by Mary Baker as they had Princess Caraboo) paid for a ticket so that she could set sail to America and continue her ruse.

She successfully travelled with a circus sideshow for a few months but was eventually exposed in the States too, whereupon she returned to Bristol and lived out the rest of her years as a Bedminster leech seller.

When she died, she was penniless and interred in a pauper's grave somewhere in this small cemetery. In 1994 a Hollywood film retelling her life (which, is both surprisingly good and surprisingly accurate) starring Phoebe Cates was released. There was a promise by the film studio that if the movie was a commercial success, they would pay for a headstone for Mary Baker. Sadly, it was a box office flop and Princess Caraboo's grave remains unmarked.

Though she may have died a pauper, Mary Baker managed to dine with aristocracy and to see the world. Even if her grave has been lost, she will forever be remembered as an audacious woman who managed to do the impossible.

*For the next stop, return to North Street and continue on towards Raleigh Road (in front of the Tobacco Factory.) At the far end of Raleigh Road where it meets Beauley Road, there is an interesting sculpture of a man's face on one of the buildings.*

## 9. The Wills Roundel

On a building at the intersection of Beauley Road and Raleigh Road there is an unusual looking sculpture of a man's head surrounded by a circle. This type of sculpture is known as a roundel, and this particular one has a fair amount of mystery surrounding it.

It's believed to date back to about 1890 and is thought to have been made from the terracotta that had been salvaged from a tobacco factory which was built nearby but was demolished to make way for a larger tobacco building.

Both the sculptor of this roundel and the subject remain a mystery, but many people agree that because of the material used, and the area in which it was installed, it is most likely intended to depict Henry Overton Wills (1761-1826) - not to be confused with his eldest son, who had the same name.

H.O. Wills senior became the part-owner of a small tobacco shop in central Bristol in 1786 and immediately began profiting from the sale of cigarettes, believing that he could manufacture good quality products which were available at a cost that would suit the meagre fortunes of the average Bristolian.

Soon, Wills had expanded his business across the city and demand for his cigarettes became nationwide (and eventually global). When his sons took over the business following his death, they saw south Bristol, and particularly the small, rural parish of Southville as the most promising location to expand their enterprise into, and soon their business was among the most profitable in the city with a series of factories peppering the area south of the New Cut.

With the expansion of the business came the inevitable call for housing in the area. Wills Tobacco was far and away the largest employer in the city but most of its workers lived on the other side of Bristol, so the solution was to develop the land around the factories into a series of interlocking terraced streets, which began construction around the middle of the 19th century.

The Wills family were Quakers and had long been associated with the temperance movement in Bristol, but interestingly, none of them are believed to have been smokers. The reason for this may seem unclear, as it was many decades later that an association between smoking and poor health was definitively proven.

The speculation seems to be that while the Wills family may have personally seen smoking as detrimental to one's health, or even as an unpleasant vice, they also believed in an individual's liberty to make decisions for themselves - of course, this opinion was likely bolstered by the fact that they were financially benefitting for the sale of tobacco.

Far stricter, however, were their opinions on drinking, which they saw as a dangerous habit which lessened the quality of life for all the people of the city. For this reason, the entirety of the complex of streets they funded for their tobacco factory workers was built without a single pub.

We can only wonder what they would make of the Tobacco Factory today - one of the most popular drinking establishments in south Bristol!

*Stay on Beauley Road and follow it northwards towards the New Cut. Our next stop is at the junction of Beauley Road with Coronation Road.*

## 10. The Feral Chickens of Southville

Coronation Road is the pleasant terrace street overlooking the New Cut, running the length of what most people regard as Bedminster and Southville. Traditionally, it has appealed to the wealthier families of south Bristol, but for some time, it's also been rumoured to be home to a handful of very unlikely residents.

Since about the mid-late 1980s, there have been rumours of chickens being sighted along the road and its adjoining neighbourhoods. Most of the time, these birds have been spotted along the grassy embankment which meets the New Cut but there have even been tales of them brazenly wandering about the streets.

If they exist at all, the obvious question is, where did they come from? The most likely origin seems to be Windmill Hill City Farm near Victoria Park. The farm was established in 1976 by a group of volunteers who wanted to create a working farm in urban surroundings which could help teach city-dwelling children how food is produced.

Chickens have been part of the farm's history since almost the very beginning, and it's certainly plausible that a few could have escaped unnoticed, but it could be just as likely that the chickens were escapees from private gardens where they were being kept for their eggs.

What would make the feral chickens all the more remarkable is not just how they've managed to evade detection for so long, but also how they've managed to survive against those two formidable foes to hen-welfare: traffic and Bristol's huge fox population.

When the chickens first made an appearance, it was during the period of the 1980s when the city was undergoing a mange problem among its foxes. It's estimated that over 90% of Bristol's foxes died during this time, so if a population of hens were going to make an appearance, this would have been the time to do it. As for evading the cunning foxes' teeth and appetites, the best theory seems to be that while foxes hunt at night, chickens roost in trees.

A further rumour suggests that there has only ever been one feral chicken on Coronation Road. A wily creature who seems very good at hiding and has been inevitably named "The Coronation Chicken". One story even claims that this bird once attacked a man who was walking home from the pub in order to steal his chips - unsurprisingly, this story has never been verified.

So could a lone chicken have survived for so long? She'd need to be at least thirty years old if she was the only one to have escaped captivity. The oldest hen ever recorded lived to be sixteen years old, so it seems that if the contemporary sightings of chickens are to be believed, we must be dealing with a small brood of breeding hens, which then leads to a further question. How did these hens find a rooster?

Could the legend of the feral chickens be true? Possibly, but it's hard to imagine that the sightings have all been of the same batch of escapees from the 1980s, so the next time you find yourself walking along the New Cut late at night, guard your chips well, for who knows when the Coronation Chicken will strike again?

*Thats the end of our wander through south Bristol. The next stage is a very challenging but rewarding one, which take us all the way to the Downs. Cross over Vauxhall bridge - the pedestrian Bridge further west down Coronation Road, then head through the housing estate until you find the Floating Harbour. Around here there is a rounded statue on a plinth. Although this statue has no plaque informing you so, it is named "Atyeo" and will be the first stop on our next trail.*

# Walk Four
## Up The Hill

# Up the Hill

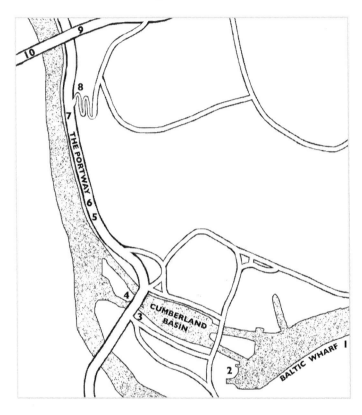

The next walk on our tour includes by far the most difficult section - the Zig Zag Path, but it will also take you through some of the lesser known and almost forgotten history.

From wrecked ships to one of Brunel's hidden gems, this walk has a slightly industrial emphasis, but there's still room to hear a tale of a lovelorn giant, Georgian exercise rituals and of course, no trip around our city would be complete without a visit to the Clifton Suspension Bridge - Bristol's most iconic structure.

# 1. Atyeo

Baltic Wharf can feel a little neglected sometimes - not because the area is in any way run down, but simply because without the nightlife or historic buildings which are a tourist draw to the central harbour, this mostly residential area can get a bit overlooked - which is a shame as it's an utterly charming and tranquil stretch of the waterway.

It takes its name from the period of the 19th century when the area was known for its shipbuilding, and the finest wood in the world for that could be found in the Baltic region. Vessels would come to Bristol loaded with small forests worth of stripped Baltic trees, which would be dragged by hand to the ship yards - this is why this part of the harbour is the only place to have sloped sides.

There are a trio of statues along this section of the waterway, and the one in the centre (opposite Westbrook Court) is named "Atyeo".

When it was unveiled in 1986, there was a great deal of derision in the local press, with one journalist scoffing that it looked like a cross between a fish and a shoe.

It was carved by Bristol-born sculptor Stephen Cox from red Verona marble - one of the densest rocks it is possible to sculpt from. Its form is meant to evoke both tremendous strength but also a fluidity of motion, these qualities were why it was given its name.

John Atyeo, whom the statue in named in honour of, was a footballer, born in Wiltshire in 1932, who spent his entire professional career playing for Bristol City.

After a couple of years as a volunteer player for Portsmouth, Atyeo came to Bristol in 1951 and was signed as a semi-professional aged just 19. From there, he went on to have a remarkable career at the club, becoming one of its most celebrated players.

It's often been argued that Atyeo would have become a player of national renown had he accepted any of the plentiful offers to transfer to other teams, but not even an offer of the modern-day equivalent of £20 million to play for Liverpool - which would have made him the most expensive player in English football - was enough for him to leave his beloved team.

In a period that was less than stellar for Bristol City, Atyeo became a one-man scoring machine for the club, racking up 30 goals between 1955 and 1956.

Clearly, Atyeo was not a man who craved the limelight, as when he retired in 1966, he sought out a career based on his other passion - mathematics. He became a maths teacher at Kingsdown School in Warminster, a post he held for twenty years.

It is not just for excellence in sport which explains this public dedication to him, (aside from Stephen Cox's tribute, there is also a statue of him outside Ashton Gate Stadium) it's also for his loyalty to his club and to Bristol, which has won him a place in the city's history forever.

*Continue following the harbour westward until you come to a ship building yard. Provided it's open, you should be able to stroll right into Underfall Yard, which is our next stop on the tour.*

## 2. Underfall Yard

The area surrounding St Augustine's Parade is often seen as being the heart of the harbour but at the west end, near Cumberland Basin, you will find the Underfall Yard - undoubtedly the harbour's brain.

Today, it is best known as a shipbuilding and restoration hub - a purpose it has fulfilled for centuries, but it also serves as an educational centre, explaining the history and multifaceted importance of the yard.

Built in 1809 to a design by engineer William Jessop, it was a vital addition to the construction of the Floating Harbour, as without it, the docks would soon have been overflowing with silt.

Jessop's plan was for a series of sluices which could filter the water coming into Bristol, so that when more of the River Avon needed to be let into the harbour, it did not bring with it an equal measure of silt. These sluices, known as the Underfalls, are where the boatyard gets its name.

Jessop also designed a series of "overfalls" which would pump excess water from the harbour to the New Cut in case of flooding, but they were never built.

In the 1830s the sluicing devise was greatly improved with the help of Isambard Kingdom Brunel, who also suggested using dredging ships in the harbour to help alleviate silt build up.

Over the years, improvements continued to be made to the Underfalls and the surrounding system of hydraulic powered locks at the west end of the harbour. By 1938, Underfall Yard was capable of powering cranes and swing bridges as far away as Redcliffe Wharf, thanks to an ingenious web of underground waterways, which used compressed water and steam to provide energy.

This whole system was eventually charged by the magnificently steam-punk Pump House, which is now open to the public, as well as the hydraulic accumulator, designed in 1954. This huge, steel barrel could be loaded with scrap metal and its combined weight would be enough to compress countless tons of water, which could then be directed from the Underfall Yard to wherever in the city it was needed.

Perhaps most remarkable of all, is that this whole system works on a combination of gravity, water pressure and steam and does so in a manner which is almost entirely clean and renewable.

It's an engineering marvel - which surprisingly few people are aware of - and a testament to generations of mavericks and geniuses, who have helped to build Bristol into the remarkable city it is today.

*Pass through Underfall Yard and continue on to the Cumberland Basin. This is our next destination.*

## 3. Cumberland Piazza: Bristol's Lost Park

Unloved and abandoned, Cumberland Basin is never spoken of as fondly as the rest of the harbour, but it's a little known fact that this was once one of the most exciting and cutting edge areas of the city.

The road system, including the flyover, was commissioned in the 1960s and was an elegant solution to one of the major problems Bristol had experienced since the rise of the car. When bridges needed to swing to allow ships into the Floating Harbour, traffic would grind to a halt and could be backed up the length of the city at busy times. This system allowed vehicles to be diverted, depending on where bridges were being swung, so that traffic flow could continue unabated when large vessels came into the city.

The centrepiece of this complex is Plimsoll Bridge, the gargantuan, movable section of the overpass which is easily the largest and heaviest swing bridge in Bristol.

Plimsoll Bridge takes its name from Samuel Plimsoll (1824-1898), the Bristol-born politician, social reformer and inventor. Had he been nothing more than an MP, Plimsoll would be remembered for little besides once receiving a formal reprimand in Parliament for shaking his fist at the Speaker, but as an inventor, he devised the Plimsoll line marker on ships which, when below the waterline, meant that the vessel was overloaded.

Overloading was a major cause of shipwrecks during the Victorian era, and the creation of this simple line (which remains in use to this day) has doubtlessly saved thousands of lives at sea.

During the 1960s, the public did not have the same reservations about the use of concrete in public parks. It was often seen as a wonder material, allowing huge scale developments to be built for a relatively small amount of money, and for that reason, it was somewhat embraced as a modernistic, possibly even futuristic advancement. Many designers of the age took advantage of the possibilities that concrete offered, and few were as influential as Sylvia Crowe, the landscape architect who was tasked with designing a park to be built around and under the overpass.

The resulting park was called Cumberland Piazza, and was regarded as one of Crowe's masterpieces at the time. Crowe believed that urban spaces should have clearly delineated areas for pedestrians and traffic, and had no qualms about mixing concrete alongside trees and flowerbeds. Later, four huge anchors were placed around the corners of the park, each salvaged from shipyards, and each pointing in the direction of a compass point, as a reminder of the city's nautical heritage.

Her park featured a cafe, a large children's play area and a network of ornate, butterfly-shaped fountains. Surviving photographs of it may seem rather brutalist and cold but we must try to imagine what it must have seemed like at the time - a completely revolutionary space which allowed families to rest by the waterside while heavy traffic passed overhead.

This trend in landscape design did not last for long. Concrete does not age attractively and soon the pristine pillars turned dark grey. The whole area began to feel rather depressing - even a little threatening.

Moreover, what people were looking for in urban parks had changed by the late sixties. People did not want to spend their leisure time surrounded by traffic and instead went in search of more natural environments in tranquil settings, and parks began to be designed more as oases from the hustle and noise of urban living.

Cumberland Piazza was soon left to become an untouched and almost abandoned corner of our otherwise beautiful harbour.

*The next stop is beneath the Plimsoll Bridge, where another bridge, made of iron tubing, can be found. This is "Brunel's Other Bridge" - or "B.O.B."*

## 4. Brunel's Other Bridge

Tucked away in a seldom visited location under Plimsoll Bridge on Cumberland Basin, slowly decaying against the elements, is an almost forgotten curio from the life of Isambard Kingdom Brunel.

Nicknamed "B.O.B." or "Brunel's Other Bridge", this iron marvel predates Brunel's most celebrated Bristol bridge by many years, being designed and completed in 1849, when the Clifton Suspension Bridge was nothing more than two towers and a financial headache for the city.

B.O.B. was constructed in the same dockyards which had built the S.S. Great Britain a couple of years before and the process appears to have been closely surveyed by Brunel himself, as he had never attempted an iron bridge of this size before.

Its innovative design, utilising cylindrical, wrought iron, may well have been an experiment by Brunel as to how stable such a construction would be. Evidently, the results were just as the man had hoped, as he went on to implement them on one of his most celebrated designs - the Tamar Bridge between Devon and Cornwall.

Another brilliant piece of engineering was its swing system, allowing the entire bridge to rotate on a central pivot which was driven by hydraulic pressure and could allow passage into the harbour of two boats at once.

The bridge was another triumph for Brunel who, by this time, was proving himself to be one of the most ingenious engineers of his age, and it remained in use for over a century as the primary means of crossing the docks. It was only closed in 1960, when Plimsoll Bridge was completed. The bridge was permanently swung open and left abandoned.

Despite its nickname, Brunel's Other Bridge isn't the only other Brunel bridge in Bristol (aside from the obvious one, of course). Over the River Avon, towards Temple Meads there is a stone bridge that was completed to Brunel's design in 1839. Sadly, this bridge is almost impossible to view properly as it's on a very inaccessible stretch of the river, worse still is that it was subsequently widened with girder bridges on either side, nearly obscuring Brunel's original construction entirely.

These two unsightly girder bridges flanking the stone bridge have given it the nickname "the Cinderella Bridge" as its humble beauty is masked by two ugly stepsisters!

B.O.B. is on a list of at-risk heritage sites and its future is uncertain. In order to restore and protect this ailing masterpiece, a large sum of money must be spent. Though Bristol is a city that's never flushed with spare cash, I really do hope that the society which was founded in the 1970s to save this historic marvel have success, because it would be a travesty to see this beautiful and important feat of engineering turn to rust.

*Go past the locks and follow the River Avon on the left side of the Portway, when you come to some dilapidated looking wooden platforms built high above the river, you have reached the next destination.*

## 5. The Hotwells Jetties

Depending on when you're reading this, the wooden jetties that can be found just outside of the harbour at Hotwells may have been demolished.

For a long time there have been plans to remove them as they're somewhat at risk of collapse, which, though an understandable concern, in losing these jetties, we will risk losing an interesting part of our history.

The ones which are currently standing weren't built until the 1930s and replaced ones that had been built in the 1860s. Technically, they are wharfs, as they are not built flush against the wall, but are referred to by just about everyone as jetties - so I'll be doing the same.

It's an often forgotten fact that Hotwells once rivalled Bath as a destination for fashionable Georgians, eager to soak in naturally occurring spas (the name Hotwells is even derived from the hot wells that have been found here since at least the 9th century.)

Bath remained popular while Hotwells did not for one very simple reason - the water in the spas was discovered to be incredibly toxic, but enough time had passed for Hotwells' reputation to be illustrious enough that it continued as a popular attraction for high society, and the jetties were originally built for steam ships to bring day trippers to the popular district.

Later, they were somewhat repurposed to allow for travel in the other direction. With the construction of the funicular Clifton Rocks Railway in 1893 (more info on that in Walk Six) the people of Clifton now had immediate access to the River Avon and steam ships began taking the people of the prestigious suburb on trips to Clevedon and Cardiff, or sometimes even just to bob around in the Bristol Channel for a while.

Often the destination wasn't all that important, because the true purpose of these trips was not always sightseeing. The steam ships were able to operate under maritime law once in the Bristol Channel, meaning that on Sundays they were permitted to sell alcohol.

Similar services were offered on Sundays from the Floating Harbour, most notably, MV Balmoral, which can still be seen near the M Shed Museum, offered a cut-price route out of the city for those on a lower budget, which was still in operation during the 1960s.

During WWII, steamships were conscripted as part of the war effort and the Clifton Rocks Railway made way for a secret BBC broadcasting station (and bomb shelter) and the Hotwells jetties began falling apart without proper maintenance.

By the end of the war, trends had changed among the social elite, who now largely owned cars, and were able to plan day trips to destinations of their choosing, and had little use for the steamships. This, coupled with a loosening of Sunday drinking laws, meant the services from Hotwells ceased forever, and the jetties continued their slow, sad decay.

*You're pretty much at our next stop already, as it will concern a legend of the Gorge's creation. As long as you can get an impressive view of the gorge, then anywhere around here will make a suitable location.*

## 6. The Giants of the Gorge

For as long as we've had written records, and probably even longer than that, Britain has been home to countless myths and legends, but few are as sad as the tale of heartbreak which befell a noble, yet lazy, giant named Goram.

A version of the story seems to originate from the 16th century but the most popular retelling of it was penned by the boy poet, Thomas Chatterton (for more information, he is featured in Walk Two).

It seems unlikely that anybody was actually meant to believe this story of how the Avon Gorge and various other geographical oddities around Bristol came to be formed, but it was part of a tradition of the age to create fanciful, romantic legends of local topography. The most popular retelling of the story goes like this:

In ancient times, a pair of brothers named Goram and Vincent, who just happened to also be giants, spent their lives on the barren, flat wasteland that would eventually become Bristol.

One day, the two brothers met a beautiful maiden named Avona, who they both immediately fell in love with. In most versions of the story, she too is a giant, but in some alarming variants she is a regular-sized human woman.

Avona, not wanting to choose between the brothers, instead set a challenge for them. She offered her hand in marriage to whichever of the giants could bring flowing water to the arid land. The two brothers wasted no time and set about digging channels through the rocky landscape.

Vincent, the larger of the two, broke his way through what would become the Avon Gorge towards the Bristol

Channel, while Goram worked a passage through Hazel Brook in Henbury.

It was tiresome work for Goram, who decided to allow himself a rest. He punched a chair into the cliff face of his newly formed gorge and then promptly fell asleep.

When he awoke, he realised to his horror, that his brother had not only met Avona's challenge and that water was flowing across the land, but that she was now betrothed to Vincent.

Heartbroken, Goram stomped his foot into the ground and cursed his laziness, ran all the way to the Bristol Channel, flung himself into the waters and drowned. The islands of Flat Holm and Steep Holm are, according to the legend, his head and shoulder.

In Blaise Castle Estate, where Hazel Brook can be found, a strange rock formation over the gorge is said to be Goram's Chair, while a flattened ditch is claimed to be where the devastated giant stamped his foot.

Although Vincent is remembered as the giant who dug the Avon Gorge, most of the legends are sympathetic to poor Goram, who became the subject of countless ballads during the Georgian era, while Vincent, the victor, was the subject of none.

Perhaps it is the nature of Bristolians to favour the underdog or, perhaps, Goram is simply a reminder to us all of the ravages of a broken heart.

*The next stop takes us a little further along the Portway. Just before you reach the section of the road which is covered by a concrete tunnel, you should be able to look up the river and see the first large bend. This will be the subject of our next stop.*

# 7. The Wrecked Ships of the Avon

Crossing the oceans had been a perilous voyage for centuries, but throughout Bristol's nautical history, one of the most dangerous stretches of water was the serpentine River Avon.

The vast tidal range of the river, coupled with its hidden sandbanks and unexpected currents has meant that timing and careful planning have been of utmost importance to vessels arriving or departing the city.

The most perilous section of the Avon is Horseshoe Bend, a lethally tight curve in the river, which also happens to be a point where it is at its shallowest. This channel has seen the end of countless ships that have misjudged their approach and run aground - oftentimes preventing other vessels from entering or leaving the harbour for several days.

Horseshoe Bend has also been responsible for limiting the size of ships which can come into port. When the SS Great Britain was built in 1841, it was not only the largest ship in the world, but also the largest ship capable of being made in Bristol, as even though the locks on the Floating Harbour were completely rebuilt to accommodate the scale of the "Grand Lady" - were she any larger, there would have been no chance of steering her through the tight bend.

The obvious solution would seem to be one of destroying the sandbanks - an approach which was attempted several times, using both man power and explosives but infuriatingly it appears to be the shape of the river itself which leads to deposits building up, and no matter how quickly you attempt to rid the river of the silt, within hours it reforms.

This imposing obstacle was what eventually put an end to Bristol's years as an international port. With the construction of Avonmouth Docks, large ships could avoid travelling upriver to Horseshoe Bend altogether, so there was no longer any need to deliver cargo to the city.

The most expensive ship ever to wreck in the Avon was also the second largest in the world - and it happened on her maiden voyage.

The SS Demerara was a Steamship, built in Bristol and the second largest ship ever built. On the 10th of November 1851, she was due to be guided through the Avon Gorge by a tugboat, after which she was headed to Scotland to be fitted with ocean-faring motors.

The tugboat, however, had misjudged its timing by a matter of minutes and the tide was getting perilously low. Rather than wait for a higher tide, the skipper of the tug attempted instead to head through the river at top speed (about nine knots). This was to prove a calamitous mistake.

The SS Demerara began swaying erratically in the tugboat's wake and by the time the ship was close to passing below where the Clifton Suspension bridge is now (then just two towers on either side of the gorge) she was travelling almost diagonally through the water. She ran aground on a sandbank and immediately broke almost entirely in two.

There was no hope of ever re-floating her and she was dismantled at the scene. For three days, river access was blocked until all of her parts could be removed.

Parts of the SS Demerara were later used to construct a ferry, less than half of the ship's original size. This disastrous launch was so alarming that it almost completely stopped large-scale ship building in Bristol for a couple of years.

A replica of a relic from this wreck can still be viewed today. When the ship was being dismantled, one of the workers was eagle-eyed enough to salvage the ship's figurehead - a representation of a native American man. For many years this was visible over the entrance to a shop on Small Street (now Colston Street). Eventually it became too decayed, and was replaced by a replica which was later purchased by a business on Augustine's Parade where it can still be seen today - above the Drawbridge Pub near the Hippodrome.

*I suggest plenty of water for the next stage. The tour is about to take you up an enormous climb to Clifton, via the Zig Zig Path. The entrance to it is behind a stone wall on the opposite side of the road.*

## 8. The Zig Zag Path

The Zig Zag Path leading from the Portway all the way up to the Clifton Suspension Bridge Viewing Point is quite possibly one of the most challenging to be found in all of Bristol.

It's existed in some form since at least the 1780s as a means of connecting two of the most prestigious neighbourhoods of the time, Hotwells and Clifton. The Georgians were particularly keen on health fads, mostly dietary but sometimes incorporating exercise too, and one of the most popular was the idea of a morning "constitutional" - a walk uphill to be taken before breakfast.

The Zig Zag Path is believed to have served such a purpose, along with another hill running between the two suburbs - unsurprisingly known as "Constitution Hill". At one point you may have spotted any number of red faced Georgians attempting to conquer this audacious hill without even the aid of a hearty breakfast.

A morning constitutional was still being prescribed well into the Victorian era but by that time, Zig Zag Hill had been rebuilt and repurposed as a means of getting material from ships on the river, all the way up to where the Clifton Suspension Bridge was being built.

A journey straight up the hill could have been enough to kill a horse if it had a heavy load in tow, but it had long been known that horses could be driven up even impossibly steep climbs if the path was laid out in a more leisurely zig-zag.

It worked and throughout much of the bridge's active construction years, a steady train of horses would be guided up and down throughout the daylight hours.

Nowadays, the Zig Zag Path is used for its health benefits and is a popular challenge for cyclists. If you do feel fit enough to attempt it, you will not be disappointed, as if you make it to the top, the view is (literally) breathtaking!

*Congratulations if you made it to the top! We're not quite finished going uphill (sorry) but it's a much more sedate climb. Our next stop is the tower of the Suspension Bridge on the Clifton side.*

# 9. Building a Masterpiece

The Clifton Suspension Bridge is easily our most beloved icon. Recognised the world over as one of the most beautiful bridges ever made, it is often regarded as Brunel's greatest achievement - and one he never lived to see completed.

While it's impossible to imagine the city without the bridge, it's incredible to think that it almost never happened.

There were plans to build a bridge across the gorge since 1753. Businessman William Vick left a sum of £1,000 in his will to fund such a structure, which he hoped would be his legacy to the city. This was the modern-day equivalent of about £140,000.

Several plans were put forward over the following years, most notably William Bridges' mind-bogglingly gigantic bridge, which was essentially constructed of houses stacked upon one another as a kind of city within a city.

Stone had been the only material ever used to construct bridges even close to the length it would need to be in order to cross the gorge, and all estimates of building such a crossing ran into millions of contemporary pounds.

By 1829, interest had raised Vick's endowment to £8,000 and soon people were wondering if now was the time for the money to be spent. The following year a contest was held between engineers to design a bridge which could cross the gap at a cost-effective price.

Dozens of entries were submitted to the committee which was overseen by bridge-building maestro Thomas Telford, who promptly dismissed all the others and declared his own the winner.

This enraged a young Isambard Kingdom Brunel, whose own submission had been snubbed. In response, he handed the committee the design of a bridge that he claimed could be built at a fraction of the cost of Telford's.

The design was unlike anything anyone had seen before. A huge, single span suspension bridge, held aloft not by a central pillar but by nothing more than the strength of the cables.

A single span bridge of this length had never been attempted before, and many people, including Isambard's own father, engineer Marc Brunel, believed it was impossible for the project to work.

Nevertheless, he was declared the final winner of the contest and work was soon underway, beginning with the firing of an arrow with a trailing wire from the Clifton side of the gorge into Leigh Woods. This wire would hang over the gorge for over thirty years.

The bridge hit trouble almost immediately when work was suspended by the Bristol riots and as the project stalled investors began to get nervous, many of them pulling out their money. By 1843, the funds had dried up entirely and the bridge was nothing but a pair of sombre towers overlooking Bristol.

Brunel died in 1859 and work resumed soon afterwards, now more in tribute to the man than anything else. Buoyed by public donations and government funding, the bridge was completed with the help of a pair of chains which had been salvaged from the rebuilding of Brunel's own Hungerford Bridge in London.

The plans were also somewhat adjusted from the original, with the help of William Henry Barlow and Sir John Hawkshaw - whose names appear alongside Brunel's on one of the towers.

The span was finally completed in 1864, after 33 years of construction. It had been a long, infuriating and costly affair, but the city fell in love with its magnificent bridge at once. Bristol now had an icon not just for its time, but for time immemorial.

*If you have a head for heights, I recommend a stroll across the bridge to the other side to read the second installment on the Clifton Suspension Bridge, if not, I recommend staying where you are for more tales of the bridge.*

## 10. Firsts for the Bridge

This section is a little different to the others. We all know that when it first opened, the Clifton Suspension Bridge held the records for highest and longest single-span bridge in the world, but there were other firsts too, and I want to talk about them.

When the bridge opened in December 1864, a crowd of over 100,000 people attended the ceremony. There had been speculation about who would be the very first member of the public to cross (construction workers had, obviously, done this many times before) and it had been proposed that it might be decided by a raffle. However, to the dismay of many, a handful of notable Bristolians, mostly associated with the Lord Mayor's Office and the Society of Merchant Venturers, were to be the first to have the honour.

One person in the crowd who was not happy with this arrangement was a 21 year old Hanham barmaid named Mary Griffiths, who managed to elbow her way through before sprinting full pelt across the bridge. Upon reaching the other side, she became the very first person officially recognised as having crossed the span.

A somewhat more daring first was for Duty Pilot Officer F. G. Wayman, who, in 1927, accepted a wager to pilot an aeroplane under the bridge. He accomplished the feat to the astonishment of onlookers but was given a severe reprimand from his army base. It is said that he spent his entire winnings on beer.

Thirty years later, perhaps to celebrate the anniversary, Flying Officer Crossley attempted the same stunt. Though he did successfully pilot his aircraft under the bridge, three decades of flight technology advancements had greatly increased the speed of aeroplanes and he subsequently lost control of the craft, crashing into the Leigh Woods side of the gorge and dying instantly.

It cannot be ignored that the Clifton Suspension Bridge has had a notorious reputation for suicides. Before prevention barriers were installed in the 1990s, it was possibly second only to Beachy Head for those poor souls for whom life was simply too much.

The first incident of somebody dying by suicide on the bridge happened less than 18 months after it opened, when George Green took his life in 1866, beginning a dark and tragic tradition.

In 1885, Sarah Ann Heney jumped from the bridge after her boyfriend split up with her. The devastated young woman became the first of only a handful of people to survive the terrible fall, thanks to her impressively buoyant petticoats slowing her descent. She made a full recovery and went on to live a rich and full life until the age of 85.

It was for jumpers of a different sort on April Fools Day, 1979 that the bridge was the scene of another first. Four members of the Dangerous Sports Club - a group who committed acts of derring-do in public places - attached elasticated ropes around their waists and leapt from the bridge, bouncing several times before the ropes went taught, whereupon they paused to dangle over the gorge while drinking champagne.

This incredibly dangerous stunt earned them all fines from the court but it is now recognised as the very first occurrence in Britain of what would come to be known as bungee-jumping.

*If you want to continue onto the next walk, which concerns the history, prehistory and natural history of the downs, from the bridge, follow the hill beside Bridge Road towards the Observatory, which will be where the walk begins.*

# Walk Five
## Up On The Downs

# Up on the Downs

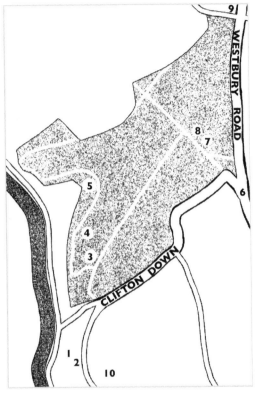

This walk will take us on a stroll across one of our oldest, largest and most popular green spaces.

A couple of locations (3 and 4) aren't specifically about the places you'll be stopping off at if you choose to do this tour, because the subjects they cover, involve all of the Downs as an area, but I think I've chosen suitably impressive vistas to look out over as tales from Bristol's history and pre-history are recounted.

On this walk, you'll hear, among other things, about ancient life both here and across Bristol, a merciless highwayman with an evil scheme - who's still said to haunt the area, and a humble toilet attendant - who wrote one of the most scandalising books on Bristol in history.

# 1. The Observatory

One of the most distinct sights from the Clifton Suspension Bridge is not to be found in the city far below, but by looking across to the odd, cylindrical building on a little hill overlooking the bridge. This is the Clifton Observatory, and it has a weird story to tell.

Though it's currently used to house a camera obscura - a fascinating contraption which projects a panorama of the surrounding area onto a concave screen - it was originally built in 1766 as a windmill to grind corn. It served this function for a couple of years before it was slightly converted to help feed the city's insatiable need for snuff powder. It operated as one of Bristol's most active snuff mills until one night almost a decade later.

Who was responsible for locking the mechanism which would prevent the sails from turning has been lost to time, but whoever it was, forgot to do so on the night before Halloween 1777.

Unbeknownst to the city, a huge storm was on the way and when it reached Bristol, it sent the windmill sails spinning so fast that the friction it caused was enough for a spark to ignite some sacks of snuff which had been stored there for the evening. Snuff, like many fine powders, can be highly flammable and within minutes the entire windmill was ablaze and completely gutted soon afterwards. Everything wooden in the building was destroyed, leaving only the round stone walls intact.

The windmill remained unused and a sad wreck on the hill for many years. It had been owned by the Society of Merchant Venturers - a sort of business club for the wealthy of Bristol, which still operates today - who had struggled to find a use for the burnt out shell, but didn't want to lose such an attractive building.

In 1828, a local artist named William West asked the Merchant Venturers if he could install a studio in the building, hoping the views over the gorge would encourage him to paint, and the men agreed.

His studio and artwork became very popular and soon he was offering tours of the building, which he had fully renovated and decorated with world maps and his own artwork, as well as fitting a powerful telescope in the domed roof.

Hoping to inspire others to see the natural beauty of the Avon Gorge, William West constructed the camera obscura, which allowed aspiring artists to study the geological marvel in detail and even dug through the basement so it could meet a naturally occurring cave that overlooked the river from a dizzying height.

West's keen eye for beauty and love of the natural world truly did inspire visitors to his studio, and the Clifton Observatory, as it's now known, became a piece of art in its own right during his stay there. It continues to enchant and inspire people today, which is precisely what I think the artist would have hoped for.

*Stay close to the Observatory. Along the eastern edge of the field you should be able to see some ridges, just before the hill slopes downward. Head over towards them.*

## 2. Bristol Before Bristol

Along the eastern edge of the hill upon which the Clifton Observatory stands, it's possible to see a few peculiar ridges running through the grass. These may not at first look like much, but they are evidence of some of the earliest stone dwellings in Bristol.

This was once a settlement for the Dobunni tribe of England. As with all ancient tribes not a great deal is known about them, but their settlements can be found in locations around an area which generally matches the county of Bristol.

This settlement (and a similar one in Leigh Woods) are among the oldest of the Dobunni tribe, dating back to around 1200 BC, the dawn of the Iron Age - the last of the great epochs of human development after the Stone Age and Bronze Age.

Although these may be the only settlements to have survived in any form until the present day, there is evidence that people have lived in the area for a great deal longer.

In Shirehampton, tools and earthenware pots dating back to as much as 400,000 years ago are not only the oldest archaeological relics ever found in Bristol but are among the oldest in Britain.

We know next to nothing of how these people lived domestically, as their homes were likely made of wood and left no trace, but the startling abundance of prehistoric artifacts found in the area suggests that at one point, this corner of Bristol was once quite a major settlement for early Britons.

One theory for the scarcity of human bones found in the locations is that whoever these people may have been, they may not have buried their dead but rather floated them away on rivers.

Humans are not the only prehistoric life to have found a home in Bristol. Aside from the Downs bone fissure, which I'll talk about later on this walk, the entire city and its surrounding area was once teeming with a very special little dinosaur.

Aeons before humans evolved, Bristol was a vast marshland and was home to the thecodontosaurs, or socket-toothed lizard, one of the earliest dinosaurs to ever be discovered and named. This omnivorous reptile was not much larger than a great dane and wandered the marshes in enormous herds. It was found in such huge numbers that it's often nicknamed "The Bristol Dinosaur".

Further cementing the thecodontosaurus' place as the city's own dinosaur is that, although its population was massive, it seems to have been almost entirely based within the limits of what we would now call the county of Bristol.

*With the gorge on your left, follow the path around the Observatory to where it leads you downhill towards a road named Clifton Down. From here, take a left turn onto the Downs and head uphill onto Ladies Mile.*

### 3. The Bristol Whitebeam

Whenever you find yourself out walking on the Downs - the oldest public green space in Bristol, keep your eye out for a very unusual plant. *Sorbus bristoliensis* - the Bristol Whitebeam.

This beautiful shrub (often incorrectly referred to as a tree) is a subspecies of whitebeam that blossoms with beautiful, delicate white flowers each spring. Not only is it an important pollinator for local bees, it is also a very special plant for the city as well - as this charming shrub can only be found on the Downs, the Avon Gorge, Leigh Woods and nowhere else on Earth.

There are about a hundred examples of the Bristol Whitebeam to be found in the city and conservation efforts seem to be helping, as their numbers have steadily increased over the past decades. The Downs are the easiest place to spot them and they are dotted about sporadically across the sprawling park. Once you are able to recognise them, you'll soon realise that they were hiding in plain sight all the time.

If the Bristol Whitebeam seems like a rare breed, it is nothing compared to another plant that can be found on the Leigh Woods side of the gorge.

Discovered in 2005 by botanist and rock climber Libby Houston, the Houston's Whitebeam is a crossbreed of the Bristol Whitebeam with a more generic subspecies of the plant, and this specimen, (which grows in an area of the gorge accessible only by skilled rock climbers) is the only known example to exist in the world.

The staggeringly rare plant life around the Downs doesn't end there. If you walk along the gorge side of the park, you may be lucky enough to spot examples of the Bristol Onion and Bristol Rock Cress - both native to nowhere else but the gorge.

One of the first people to understand the importance of protecting these rare plants was none other than Isambard Kingdom Brunel who, when work began on his suspension bridge, ordered that all native plants which would be unearthed by building works, be re-planted along the gorge.

This was one of the earliest examples of environmental conservation and it helped spark a movement that sought to protect the botanical rarities of the Avon Gorge which continues to this day.

One of the most startling and unlikely environmental efforts are the gully goats, which can be found in a small valley which runs through the Downs.

A herd of five goats has been keep here for many years, and these animals have been diligently chewing their way through invasive grasses (and fertilising the land) ever since.

No visit to the Downs should be complete without a visit to see the goats, but make sure you keep your distance. Unlike farm goats, which are used to the presence of humans, these are semi-wild animals and are very shy and prefer to be left in peace!

*We're heading towards the gully where the goats can be found, but first we'll follow the edge of gorge around the Downs on our left. Wherever you can get a good view over the park will be a good place to stop.*

## 4. Jenkins Protheroe

Travelling to Bristol from any direction has been a risky affair for much of the city's history. From the 16th until well into the 19th century, it was surrounded on all sides by mile upon mile of open landscape, crisscrossed with dirt tracks and dark woodland. It was the haunt of muggers and the dreaded highwaymen, eager to rob travellers of all their worldly goods.

Few people coming to Bristol would have heard of Jenkins Protheroe - the most feared highwayman of them all, for if they had, they would never have fallen for his evil scheme.

Though the records from that time were mostly lost during WWII, there are still some written accounts of that strange era between 1775 and 1783, when Jenkins Protheroe roamed the wilderness.

Described as having a hideously malformed face and standing only a little over three feet tall (it has been suggested that he may have had a form of dwarfism), Protheroe was of no imposing stature, but what he lacked in height, he more than made up for in wicked cunning.

It's believed he operated on moonlit nights, particularly taking advantage of a full moon so that he could be seen. He would lie at the edges of paths across the Downs, where he would cry like a small child, attempting to lure weary travellers to his aid.

When a kind-hearted samaritan stopped to help what appeared to be a stricken child, he would slash at their heels with a knife - and often follow it up with a stab to the heart. Protheroe was now free to plunder the dying victim of all their material goods before slipping off into the night, leaving them to bleed to death.

Some of his victims did, however, survive this terrifying ordeal, and word soon spread across the city that a devilish man had concocted this nightmarish plan.

He was finally caught in 1783, after potentially dozens of attacks, and was convicted on multiple counts of murder. So extraordinarily evil were these crimes, it was deemed that no ordinary punishment would suffice.

He was hanged on Pembroke Road (then known as Gallows Hill) and his body was coated in tar and wrapped in chains, to swing from a gibbet over the road as a warning to other would-be criminals.

People living near this frightful scene soon complained that the sight of the dead and decaying body was simply too hideous, even more horrifying were the tales that on moonlit nights, Protheroe would spring to life and climb down from the gibbet to wander through the streets. After several weeks, the body was removed and buried in unconsecrated ground outside of the city.

How many people died by Protheroe's hand remains a matter of debate, as does some of the more sensational aspects of the story, with some researchers claiming that the tale has become as much folklore as true history with subsequent generations elaborating on the story with each retelling.

Whatever the truth, it is still said that if you visit Pembroke Road on the night of a full moon, you might just see the ghost of Jenkins Protheroe, wandering the dark and quiet streets.

*Continue on the path with the gorge to your left until you reach the entrance to the gully. Near here you should be able to spot two rounded stones which look a little like gravestones. This is our next destination.*

## 5. The City Boundary

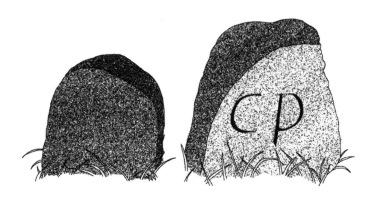

Dotted across the Downs are at least four city boundary markers - I say at least, because the exact number is unknown as large portions of the area were given over to scrubland in the 1920s and it's believed that more of them may be hidden among the undergrowth.

Taking the form of two upright stones beside one another and standing about a foot in height, these granite markers are of an unknown age but they may date back to the 17th century, when an imaginary line across the Downs marked the boundary of the city.

The "C.P." markings represent the Civil Parish of Bristol while the other represents Gloucestershire. For most of the city's history, these were little more than the boundary of each location's authority, but during the later years of the plague, markers such as these were extremely important.

Bristol was frequently quarantined from its neighbouring counties during outbreaks of the disease, which meant that nobody could enter or leave the city for months. Aside from the risk of falling ill, there was also the very real worry of starving to death if you ran out of food. The solution was for local farmers to come to the markers and leave food for the people of Bristol during the night. The following morning Bristolians would leave money.

You may wonder why Bristol's residents didn't just take the food without paying, but the thinking was simple. The farmers would not return with more food if you chose to be selfish.

Though there are no specific accounts of this exchange happening on the Downs, it was one of the places it likely occurred due to its location. Perhaps the most famous place where this is known to have happened is Pitch and Pay Lane in Stoke Bishop.

The road takes its unusual name from the times of the bubonic plague, when farmers would "pitch" their goods over the ancient wall which runs its length, and the grateful recipients would "pay" by throwing money in return.

One of these markers is near to the entrance of the gully where the wild goats roam and another is within sight of the water tower. I'll leave finding the locations of the other two down to you, as it's a fun adventure to spend an afternoon hunting them down!

*Cut across the Downs until you reach the top of Blackboy Hill. There you should find a green, iron structure on a paved island that's surrounded by roads on all sides.*

## 6. The Victorian Pissoir

Before I say anything else, I wish to dispel an oft-repeated myth about Blackboy Hill, where the ornate gentleman's convenience that will be subject of this chapter is located. It's assumed that the hill and its adjoining street, Whiteladies Road are named in reference to the slave trade.

It's said that the 'white ladies" of Bristol would come here to select their "black boy" slaves. Whilst it's true that the city does have many places that are named after various slave traders - most notably Edward Colston, Blackboy Hill and Whiteladies Road take their names from very different sources.

Though there were a few African slaves in Bristol, there's no evidence at all of slave markets being held in the city, nor was it ever a common practice for English ladies to own their own slaves. Blackboy Hill is named after the Black Boy Inn, a pub which in turn was named for Charles II, who was known as the black boy owing to his dark hair, while Whiteladies Road was also named after a pub, the White Ladies Inn, which was probably in reference to a convent of nuns located nearby.

Now with that cleared up, let's turn our attention to the cast iron urinal (or pissoir as it was known) at the top of Blackboy Hill. Built by the MacFarlane ironworks company and installed in the 1880s, it is one of only a handful of Victorian pissoirs still in use today (although only for men).

A few years ago, it was voted the ugliest listed building in Britain, which is quite an unfair claim as, on closer inspection, you will discover that this is rather a handsome construction. It was built to alleviate not just the men who used it, but also a problem which all cities had to deal with - public urination.

Many of these pissoirs were built on steep hills where pubs were, because streams of urine would otherwise flow down the streets after closing time, but this one was likely located as a convenience for the nearby Downs.

The Victorian era was a lengthy one, and over the sixty years, attitudes to public behavior changed enormously. In 1840, people would not have batted an eye at someone emptying their chamber pot in the street, but with improvements to drainage, the public became much more aware of the need for sanitation, so that by 1880, conveniences such as these were being built across the country.

It is not the only pissoir in Bristol to enjoy a listed status but is the only one to remain in service. The others are located in Mina Road Park and Horfield common, a third, too rusted and weathered to be listed, can be found just off Gloucester Road.

If you are visiting the Blackboy Hill pissoir, you may be interested to note another water facility of a different kind which is located nearby.

The structure which shares the road island with the urinal is actually a very grand drinking fountain. Built in 1904, it is a memorial to Reverend Urijah Thomas, the first reverend of Redland Park Church, now the United Reform Church.

Thomas was an enormously popular holy man who oversaw his parish for 39 years. He was also a social reformer, who believed his calling was to improve the lives of the most vulnerable people in Bristol. For decades he fought on behalf of the homeless and the hungry, even championing quite radical causes for the time, such as rehabilitation for addicts instead of imprisonment, and women's suffrage.

Unfortunately, he isn't often remembered among the greats of Bristol history, but this beautiful memorial (paid for entirely through donations by the public) should go some way to ensure he is never entirely forgotten.

*We're off to visit another toilet. Head up Blackboy Hill and follow Stoke Road until you reach the huge water tower. Next to it, you will see a Victorian toilet block. This is our next stop on the walk.*

## 7. Victoria Hughes: Local Hero

Above the entrance to the ladies toilet near the Downs water tower there is a blue plaque - one of only a few placed on a public convenience in Britain.

The dedication is to Victoria Hughes and is significant not just for its unusual location, but for the extraordinary woman it celebrates.

Born into a lower middle-class family near Blackboy Hill in 1897, Victoria Rogers was the fifth of ten children born to Alfred and Ellen Rogers. As a young girl, Victoria showed a talent and love of writing, as well as an extraordinary compassion towards other people.

She married Richard Hughes, an ironmonger from Bristol, in a hasty ceremony, as he was shipped off to fight in France that very afternoon. Richard spent much of his time during WWI in the trenches, including the Battle of the Somme - one of the bloodiest battles in human history.

When he returned he did so with a number of war wounds including trench foot, which gave him a limp for the rest of his life, and almost inevitably, a case of what was then called "shell-shock" but is now recognised as post traumatic stress disorder.

Victoria Hughes had no other choice than to find work while her husband recuperated, and managed to do so nearby as a toilet attendant or "loo lady" - a job she worked at for over thirty years until her retirement.

It is here that she encountered, for the first time in her life, the sex workers of the Downs.

For at least two hundred years, the area along the Ladies Mile was notorious for prostitution (incidentally, for about the same amount of time the area colloquially called "Fairy Land" has been a cruising ground for men in search of men).

Victoria came to understand that the sex workers of the Ladies Mile used the toilets as a means to escape, not just from the cold and rain, but from the threats of violence and everyday humiliation that blighted their work.

Soon Victoria was making tea for the women and hearing their stories. She started writing a notebook so that she could keep track of the local sex workers and ensure their safety. She also offered friendly advice that was never judgmental, nor made the women feel as if she was looking down at them.

She began documenting the daily lives of the women, as well as how they came to find themselves in such a desperate situation. In later years many of these women told of how just sitting down and having a chat with Victoria over a cup of tea gave them their humanity back.

In 1977, aged 80 and a year before her death, Victoria Hughes published her memoir *"Ladies' Mile: The Remarkable and Shocking Story of Twilight Bristol."* It was an instant sensation, shocking and scandalising its readers with its frank discussions on sexuality and vice. It's now regarded as one of the most informative (and best written) accounts of hidden Bristol ever documented.

The success of her book earned her a listing in the *"Oxford Dictionary of National Biography"* - a first for a lavatory attendant, and in 2006, a blue plaque was placed over the toilet block she had worked for so many years.

*"I hope I showed some compassion,"* she wrote in her memoir. *"They in turn gave me a sort of companionship and warmth."*

*The next stop on the walk is next door at the huge water tower.*

## 8. The Downs Bone Fissure

It should be a surprise to nobody that if you were to visit Bristol 100,000 years ago, things would look quite different.

For a start there would be no Avon Gorge. It actually formed remarkably quickly (in geological terms) during the last ice age and was most likely caused by the River Avon being diverted by a glacial wall which encroached on much of Britain. This caused the river to flow over marshland, furrowing a deep channel through limestone which, after a mere few thousand years, became the breathtaking gorge we see today.

Little was known about the animals that would have been found in Bristol during this time, but that changed when, in the 1910s, the Downs Bone Fissure was discovered.

The exact date of its discovery is unknown, probably because it was found purely by accident during some building work around what is now the water tower, and at the time there was no reason to think there was anything unusual about the seam of dark earth that had been exposed.

However it was obviously of interest to somebody as it was recorded as an oddity, and a few years later, work commenced to discover just what it could be. Sections of the seam were worked at for over a decade and within it they found a remarkable record. On two separate stratums, each belonging to separate periods of history, were hundreds of bones.

The first of these - closest to the surface, was estimated to have been formed about 30,000 years ago and contained the remains of a prehistoric elephant, a hippopotamus and a lion. These were all creatures known to have favoured warm climates, but the second included a wooly rhinoceros, a bear, several wolves and two wooly mammoths - all from the ice age and up to 200,000 years old.

This astonishing discovery seems to have caused only mild excitement at the time, and the exact details were recorded somewhat haphazardly, but these finds shed light on the prehistory of Bristol and the kind of fauna which would have been abundant during two separate eras.

The reason for these mass graveyards is likely a rather gruesome one. When the Downs were mostly marshland, some unlucky animals may have found themselves trapped in deep mud, and incapable of escape, would have drowned and sank to the bottom, their bodies becoming preserved not as fossils, but bones.

The exact location of the bone fissure has been lost to time but it's likely to have been near the current water tower. Although it's claimed that the seam was entirely excavated, it is quite possible that even more evidence of prehistoric life is still buried somewhere under the Downs.

*Travel north-east across the Downs, or alternatively, return to Blackboy Hill and follow Westbury Road northwards. Either way, stop when you come to a roundabout and look for a medium sized tree which has had a section of its trunk painted white.*

## 9. The White Tree

The white tree on the Downs is the kind of thing people could pass countless times without even noticing. At first glance it looks as if the pale trunk may be a feature of its species, or even an unfortunate disease, but this humble tree is actually part of an enduring puzzle which has perplexed the city for over 175 years.

The tree is actually hand painted every few years, as part of a tradition with an unknown origin. Why continue this custom if nobody even knows why they're doing it? Well, sometimes it's just nice to have a bit of a mystery!

The first account of the tree being painted white dates back to 1840, but it may well have begun even earlier than that. The tree you see now obviously isn't that old, and is actually the third tree to serve the purpose.

The current tree is a lime which was planted in the mid-1980s. The one it replaced originated from 1951 and was an elm - and died the same way most British elm trees did in the 70s/80s - Dutch elm disease. (Incidentally, one tree which did manage to survive the epidemic - a whych elm, can be found in Castle Park). The elm was a replacement for the original tree which may have been hundreds of years old. It was felled in order to build the nearby roundabout (which is called the White Tree Roundabout).

So why this tree? Or any tree for that matter? Well, there are several theories, but all of them suggest that it was a directional marker of some sort.

One of the most popular suggestions is that a man who was prone to drinking with a friend who lived nearby, grew tired of constantly getting lost as he drunkenly wandered the Downs on his way home. His solution was to paint a tree white so it could be better seen in the half-light, as a reminder as to which house was actually his.

Another, more probable one, was that a coaching house was situated nearby and it was a marker that there was a place to stable horses (and a bed) to overnight in.

A third suggestion is that a local man, whom tales seem to have remembered only as "Mr Gardiner," enjoyed throwing lavish soirees for guests, but did not like having to wander the Downs to track them down when he realised his visitors had become hopelessly lost. The white tree was painted by him as a kind of "the party house is over here" pointer for his guests.

Whatever the explanation, it remains an enjoyable mystery, and one that has not just survived for 175 years, but has outlived the very trees it was the subject of.

*Bit of a long walk here, retracing your steps almost all the way back to the start. Only this time, when you reach Clifton Down, look out for a three-sided stone structure on a triangle of grass between The Promenade and Clifton Down Road.*

## 10. The "Cleanest" Fountain

The ostentatious drinking fountain, which can be found beside The Promenade in Clifton was built in 1872 by the Bristol firm Broad and Tucker, to a design by brothers George and Henry Godwin. Using a combination of four different types of local stone, it was influenced by the hugely popular Bristol Byzantine architectural style of the day.

What made this fountain unusual was that it was among the first to be constructed in the city with a promise that its waters were disease free.

While this may not seem to be a particularly impressive boast nowadays, the city had spent the past forty years dealing with water-borne outbreaks of cholera - and they had every reason to be wary of the cleanliness of public water sources.

The first outbreak of the dreaded disease occurred in 1832, claiming the lives of dozens of people from all quarters, but disproportionately affecting those living in the poorer areas.

The disease claimed hundreds more victims at its height during 1849, when the outbreak was deemed so severe that the local authorities offered guidelines on how to avoid contracting the illness. One of these included drinking plenty of water - the very source of the disease.

Understanding the transmission of illness was very poor during this time, and as cholera spread mostly among the poor, it was assumed (somewhat snobbishly) that unclean homes were the culprit.

It took John Snow's 1854 study into an outbreak of cholera in Soho, London to firmly establish that outbreaks of the disease could be attributed to a handful of public water pumps in the city - and a cause was found.

Those living in the poorest areas also had the most unsanitary access to water sources, so when Dr William Budd repeated Snow's study, only this time using Bristol as his case study, he found that everyone affected in South Bristol had been using the same water pump on North Street.

With a cause established, the public immediately feared water sources, with many of them choosing to drink nothing but beer instead. Over the course of several years, drainage standards around public water sources improved greatly, particularly around North Street, where it was proven that the excrement-laden water of the New Cut had been seeping into the water source.

Cholera was eventually eradicated from the city, and all of Europe found a solution to the disease which had killed millions of people over half a century.

This drinking fountain by the Downs (like most public drinking fountains it was part-funded by temperance societies) was among the first to come with a guarantee that nothing would flow from its pipes but fresh, clean water, which must have been all that its thirsty visitors could have hoped for.

*If you want to start the next walk from here, which concerns Clifton Village, continue heading south-west on Clifton Downs. When you reach the roundabout which connects to Beaufort buildings, you should be at the corner of a wooded park. Near to this corner you should see a stone sarcophagus. This will be the start of the next tour.*

# Walk Six
## Clifton Village

# Exploring Clifton

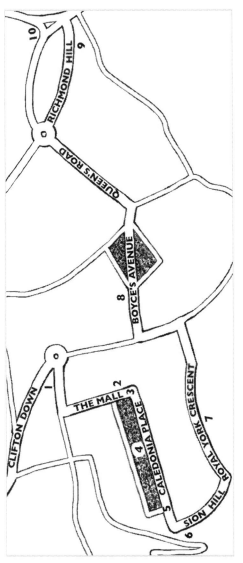

Few places in Britain have enjoyed a reputation as prestigious as Clifton, a reputation it continues to hold today, as one of our city's greatest tourist draws.

The elegant Georgian houses with their staggering views across the city have attracted the bourgeoisie for generations, but there is more to this handsome suburb - which may be older than Bristol itself, than just a playground for the rich.

This tour

will focus on some of the most fascinating people who have walked these streets, including the suffragettes, who had a meeting place nearby, the fraudulent architect who was exiled to Australia, where he became one of the nation's founding heroes, and a certain serial killer by the name of Jack the Ripper, who may have lived - and died - in Clifton Village.

# 1. The 79th Regiment of Foot Memorial

An important memorial to be found in Clifton is also one that gets consistently overlooked, but the sandstone Sarcophagus which stands at the edge of the charming leafy park at the north end of Clifton Village has a rather important place in British history.

Designed in 1767 by Thomas Paty (1713-1789), who is best remembered for having designed the current Bristol Bridge over the Floating Harbour beside Castle Park, it is a tribute to a military troop - the 79th Regiment of Foot.

The troop, formed in 1757, first saw conflict in the (now almost forgotten) Carnatic Wars, more particularly, in the third outbreak of fighting in southern India.

This lesser-known war was the result of several complex issues but can be loosely summarised as a battle between Britain and France over Indian business rights. It is generally attributed as one of the main catalysts that led to the British Raj.

Perhaps it is because of the British people's uneasiness with our history of colonialism, or because Britain's role in this conflict could be described as morally dubious at best, that this war has mostly been consigned to history books, but this understated memorial in Clifton is one of the very few monuments built as a reminder of that point in history.

What is important to remember is the very real loss of life that occurred during these wars. What is so unusual about this memorial is not just its subject matter, but that it was dedicated not to a military leader, as most of its ilk were at that time, but to the men who lost their lives in battle. It is believed that this may be the very first war memorial to be built in tribute to the ordinary people who fought and died.

138

It is overlooked by a far more grandiose construction of an obelisk. This is thought to have been designed by James Paty II, another prominent Bristol architect and nephew of the aforementioned Thomas Paty. His best-known work in Bristol is probably the Royal Fort House in Tyndall's Park.

This monument was built for William Pitt the Elder, 1st Earl of Chatham, a Whig party politician who became Prime Minister between 1766 and 1768.

Pitt was often called the "Great Commoner" because until 1766, when it was necessary to do so in order to stand for Parliament, he had refused all official titles to his name.

This pair of intriguing sculptures evoke the complexity of history and how the events and people of our past can be written out or forgotten without due care. They are important reminders that history is rarely all good or all bad - and is simply a lot more messy than we've often been led to believe.

*Head towards the Mall, the central thoroughfare of Clifton Village and follow it downhill until a narrow park appears on your right. The large building on your left will be the focus of our next chapter.*

## 2. The Fraudster's Building

About half way down the Mall there is a building which is the only legacy of an architectural mastermind to remain standing in Bristol.

The building belongs to the Clifton Club and was built around 1800 by the Mangotsfield born architect Francis Greenway (1777-1837).

The Clifton Club was a gentleman's society club (which still exists, but has admitted women since a vote in 2006). It enabled the wealthy men of the suburb to dine and socialise while discussing the affairs of the day, and of course, their various business ventures.

Francis Greenway did not have much of a head for business and had a habit of investing poorly. In 1809 he declared himself bankrupt and may even have spent a short while homeless.

Things got even worse for Greenway when, in 1812, he was arrested on charges of forgery having been accused of tampering with a legal document. The crime could carry a death sentence if he was found guilty of perjuring himself in the trial, so he was persuaded by his friends to plead guilty, in the hope of receiving a lengthy stint in prison instead.

This plan backfired on Greenway because he was sentenced to death by hanging anyway. He spent several months in Newgate Prison, roughly where the Galleries Shopping Centre stands now, to await execution.

After several months and an arduous appeal process, Greenway's sentence was lessened and he was shipped off to Australia where he would be forced to spend fourteen years as a convict.

It did not take him long to find employment in Australia, for while he was being transported a doctor aboard the ship commissioned him to build an extension to his house. In 1818, Greenway was still officially a convict but had designed half a dozen buildings in Australia, the most recent of which, the Macquarie Lighthouse, was deemed so impressive that he was awarded his freedom.

Francis Greenway is proof that no matter what happens you can't stop creative people being creative, and soon he was designing fabulous, classically inspired buildings across Australia, among them the Sydney Conservatorium of Music and the First Government House.

However, Greenway's experiences had made him no better with money and despite being highly regarded as an architect, by 1835 he was almost penniless and living off meagre handouts from friends and sympathisers. He died in 1837 of typhoid.

It was not until the 20th century that Australia began to look back on Greenway's work and appreciate it for its awe-inspiring beauty, it was around this time that he was hailed as the "Father of Australian Architecture" - and is greatly revered to this day for his contribution in establishing a nation's identity.

From 1966 until 1993, Francis Greenway's likeness was featured on the Australian $10 note - a rare tribute reserved only for those regarded as giants of Australian history. It's believed that he may be the first and only person to have both appeared on a banknote, and to have been convicted of forgery...

*In the street in front of the Clifton Club building are two extremely tall lamp posts, these are our next location on this tour.*

## 3. The Clifton Electric Lights

Standing before the Clifton Club building are two enormous lampposts. These are believed to be the first electric streetlights in Bristol.

Clifton had never struggled with public lighting. The wealthy district had been among the first to have gas lamps installed and they could be found on most streets by the 1860s. It had never seen much violent crime either - areas such as Bedminster had a serious issue with muggings during this period - but was home to only a single street light.

The installation of electric lights in Clifton was done as an experiment more than anything else. The benefits of electricity were becoming overwhelmingly clear and this cheap, yet reliable source of power had become part of very wealthy people's homes for some time.

Clifton was selected not just because it had a population who were among the most influential in the city, but because it was an area in which people had leisure time and were likely to be out doing things at night, rather than sleeping in preparation for another day of hard work.

The two lights were commissioned by the local government and were given a good deal of fanfare before they were switched on. Though some members of the public were still very wary of electricity and found it dangerously unpredictable, the switching on of the lights attracted quite a crowd and they proved to be an instant success.

The light was bright, and constant and was described by at least one overexcited onlooker as "bright as day". Soon people were travelling across Bristol to witness these marvels and demand for more of them came from all quarters of the city, and our flirtation with electricity became a full-blown affair.

While we're here, you may also be lucky enough to spy a far more natural delight. At the east end of the park which runs the length of Caledonia Place, there is a small patch of earth where a charming little flower grows. It is *lychnis chalcedonica* - also known as the Flower of Bristol.

This plant was officially adopted by the city as one of its emblems in 2006 but it has been informally recognised as a symbol of the city for over a century. The warm red colour of its flowers (which bloom throughout spring and summer) is said to have inspired the colour of the University of Bristol's crest, as well as its formal academic gowns.

*This charming park is the location of our next stop. There are entrances to it on either side.*

## 4. Clifton Mall's Mysterious Visitor

On a cold night in late November 1888, the residents living along the tranquil, twin streets of Clifton Mall and Caledonia Place were awoken by the sound of two men fighting in the park.

A pair of police officers who had been walking the beat were soon at the scene and what happened next would cause a sensation throughout the city - and yet is a chapter of our history which has almost been completely forgotten.

The two men who had been fighting were both said to be Londoners and estimated to be in their forties. One of the men was apprehended but the other managed to escape, fleeing into the night.

The man who had been caught was extremely drunk and was having trouble speaking coherently. The policemen decided that the man should be kept in a cell overnight and would have to plead his case for leniency before a magistrate the following morning.

The next day the man was brought before a judge but refused to give his name, age, or any details about himself. When told that there would be severe consequences for not doing so, he began to tell his story.

He had been a freelance journalist in the East End of London but had spent the past couple of months as a kind of amateur sleuth, attempting to catch none other than Jack the Ripper, the unknown murderer who would become the most famous serial killer in history.

At this point in time, Jack the Ripper was suspected of having killed at least seven women (some argue that there could have been as many as eleven murders, but most contemporary researchers put the number at five.) The most recent death had been Mary Kelly on the 9th of November - she is generally regarded as the last of his victims.

The man, who had still not provided his name, claimed that he had been trailing the Ripper and had followed him from the East End to Clifton, where he was now living, and that he was just about to catch the killer when the police arrived.

The magistrate declared him a fantasist and a drunk and the mysterious man was told to leave the city.

Jack the Ripper had been the talk of Britain - and indeed the world - for many months and the speculation that the killer could be living in Clifton sent ripples of fear and excitement through Bristol's high society.

Interestingly enough, artist Walter Sickert, who has long been suspected of the crimes, did spend some time in Clifton but this was many years later. Some of his artwork can be viewed in Bristol Museum and Art Gallery.

Could the man have been telling the truth and had Jack the Ripper really moved to Bristol? It's impossible to say, but an interesting footnote to the story is that a few weeks after this intriguing event, when the sensational gossip had died down, it was said that the body of a man was discovered beneath the Clifton Suspension Bridge. It was believed that he likely jumped.

The man was never identified, but there were no more Ripper murders after this body was found...

*Leave the park on the Caledonia Place side and follow the street away from the Mall until you find a series of oblong blocks on the pavement.*

## 5. The Carriage Blocks

Dotted along the lovely Clifton street of Caledonia Place are 24 oblong blocks. These are an example of my favourite sort of thing to discover while compiling Weird Bristol - the kind of thing you could walk past every day and never give so much as a second glance - but when you do look, you discover they have a hidden history of their own.

Made of pennant stone and installed along this street in the 1840s, these are what are known as "mounting blocks" and were used to assist people getting in and out of horse-drawn carriages.

During the Victorian era women were routinely bound in corsets and any number of layered clothing which greatly curtailed free movement. Like so many of the excesses of fashion through the ages, this was meant to signify one's class, as not only could someone demonstrate their wealth through the way they dressed, the sheer weight and restrictiveness of the garments identified you as someone who was not employed in any form of manual labour.

The solution to how women could gracefully enter or exit their coaches was to be found in the most illustrious areas of Bristol (and other cities). These mounting blocks would be placed to ensure women in particular (though they were used by men too) would not have to suffer the indignity of being assisted to the ground by a footman.

There are very few surviving examples of mounting blocks to be found anywhere in England. With the rise of the motor car, they were seen as taking up valuable road space and were regarded as little more than a nuisance. Later on, the fashionable areas that had first relied on them, no longer wanted them outside their homes as it implied the people who lived there could not afford cars of their own.

They seem to have remained in Caledonia Place simply because the pavements were wide enough for there to be plenty of room for pedestrians, and cars had plenty of space on the road to park.

The only other place which has a significant number of these mounting blocks is Scotland, where a concerted effort to save many of them as historical artifacts ensure they will baffle future generations.

*Continue to the western end of Caledonia Place, where you will find our next location - the upper station of Clifton Rocks Railway.*

## 6. Clifton Rocks Railway

Shuttered away behind railings, the Clifton Rocks railway is an intriguing relic from a bygone era.

With a station just off Sion Hill and another on the Portway, about 200 ft below, it is a funicular railway which once travelled through the rocks to allow the people of Clifton immediate access to the River Avon.

Constructed in 1893, passengers would use these trains during the glory years of the steamships, when ferries would take Cliftonites on day excursions out of the city. It was built incredibly quickly, using a combination of manpower and dynamite to break a tunnel through the gorge.

It was a remarkably efficient contraption, with each of the trains serving as a counterbalance to the other, with additional energy supplied by steam from oil burners.

Its day of opening was met with a great deal of fanfare and it was said that over 6,000 people rode the trains in a single afternoon. Within its first year, over half a million people had taken a trip to or from Clifton on it.

But the Victorians were hopelessly faddish and after that first year of interest in the new contraption, use of it began to dwindle. Its first year was the only time when the Clifton Rocks Railway managed to turn a healthy profit.

By 1934 the railway was still struggling to commercially support itself and its owners tried looking for someone to buy it, but its history as a financial burden was less than appealing. There were no takers and the railway was closed to the public and the trains fell silent.

It was not, however, the end of the Clifton Rocks Railway, as five years later a new purpose was found for it.

Secluded within the rocks of the gorge, it was chosen as a base for the BBC to set up a relay station. Its location meant it was literally bomb proof, so the corporation was confident that it could be transformed into a relay station, which was part of a network capable of discreetly sending (sometimes top secret) information between allies.

It also served two other functions during WWII. The first of which was as an air raid shelter. About half a dozen caves and underground sections of the gorge were repurposed in this way during the Bristol Blitz and entry to each of them was allocated to families via a lottery.

Few bombs actually fell on Clifton during the war, but Clifton College was struck twice, the latter time it seems that they were aiming for (but narrowly missed) a boarding house for Jewish boys.

The second function for the railway was to serve as a "worst case scenario" base - so that in the event of an invasion of Britain, including an overthrowing of the government - the BBC would still be able to report important information from its hidden bunker.

Mercifully for us all, this terrible event never happened.

*On Sion Hill, follow the street downwards, using the elevated pavement on the right of the road. When you get to a set of steps, follow the first down and then take another up. At the top of these steps is Royal York Crescent - and one of the most dazzling views in Bristol.*

# 7. Royal York Crescent

Royal York Crescent is, arguably, the most prestigious residential address in Bristol, and looking along the grand sweep of this Georgian street, or across the panorama of the city it overlooks, it's easy to see why.

The crescent took almost thirty years to build, partly because of funding issues but mostly it was due to the sheer scale of the project, with fifty vast houses, each built over five floors and forming a curved terrace which is over 1,000 ft long. All of it is standing on elevated paving containing storage vaults.

It's often claimed to be the longest terrace of houses in Europe - a claim that was true at the time construction was completed, but only for a short period. In 1824 the Royal Terrace in Edinburgh surpassed it by almost 100 ft.

The houses were built to be the most ornate and opulent in Clifton - which is quite a bold claim considering the architecture of the area. Servants had their own, subterranean entrances and were restricted to the basement where they worked, and an attic where they slept.

Hidden stairwells allowed access to other rooms for cleaning and serving food. It was claimed that in the most efficiently run households most of the servants would be entirely invisible to the owners of the house, so much so that were master and servant to pass each other in the street, the master would likely not even recognise the servant as a resident of his own household.

An enjoyable curiosity of Royal York Crescent isn't so much what can be found here, but what can't. For reasons which are probably less about genuine superstition than they are a desire to preserve house prices, if you follow the line of doors along the terrace, you'll notice that there is no house 13. Instead, the houses are numbered 12A and 12B.

*Follow Royal York Crescent to the western end, where it meets Regent Street. Go up the hill and take the second right onto Boyce's Avenue, at the end of which you will find the entrance to the Clifton Arcade.*

## 8. The Clifton Arcade

Though its splendour may have faded a little with time, the Clifton Arcade, tucked away down Boyce's Avenue, is an early design of what would become a revolution in shopping - and one of only a few to survive into modern times.

Opened in 1879, the high concept design of this covered shopping centre was intended to change the way Cliftonites shopped forever - and it did, in a way, eventually.

The high-end boutiques and chic emporiums of Clifton had a problem. Whenever it rained, the fashionable elite were nowhere to be found, so a solution was put forward by architect Joseph King for a self-contained high street where upscale shops would be under a single roof.

He envisioned this arcade would present shopping as an experience of its own, where people could visit, regardless of the weather, and spend an entire day. There would be areas for promenading, where women in their finest gowns could show off, and even eateries to prevent people from leaving at meal times.

His original design was considerably larger than what was eventually built. The arcade which stands today was intended to be only the first stage of a complex that would have included an elaborate pleasure garden and a larger arcade where horses and carts could be ridden through.

This was not the first such concept, but it was a first for Bristol - and among the earliest in Britain. Retailers were initially sceptical about this new approach to shopping but were lured inside by extremely competitive rental rates. By the time the arcade opened, the majority of shop space was occupied, all it needed now were the customers.

Only they didn't come. What was keeping them away was unclear, but it may simply have been an assumption that the arcade was too similar to the covered markets favoured by the middle and lower classes and the concept behind what was supposed to be a radical rethinking of the shopping experience instead felt a little tacky.

Within three months of opening, the Clifton Arcade had closed. The experiment had been an abysmal failure and it remained an abandoned shell for many years, eventually being used for little more than storage. In recent years it has been fully refurbished, alongside much needed repairs, and is now a quirky mix of funky independent clothing boutiques and art shops.

Despite being a failure, Joseph King's original concept was not abandoned. The arcade may not have been to the taste of the people of Clifton but subsequent arcades proved much more successful. The thinking behind this shopping centre was more influential than the actual building itself - as it - and other similar designs, evolved into what is now known as the modern shopping mall.

*Go through the arched building at the end of Boyce's Avenue and cross the beautiful Victoria Square. Take the first left afterwards and follow Queen's Road past the University of Bristol building until you reach a roundabout. Go right onto Richmond Hill and trail it almost to the end, where you will find the house numbered 7, which has a green plaque commemorating Sarah Guppy.*

## 9. Sarah Guppy (1770-1852)

Number 7, Richmond Hill was the final home of an unsung hero not just of Bristol, but of her age.

Born Sarah Beach in 1770, very little is known of her early life, but she married Samuel Guppy when she was 25 and the pair moved from Birmingham to Bristol that same year.

Sarah Guppy hailed from a prestigious and wealthy background, as did Samuel, and the pair were soon acquainted with the elite of the city. Eventually they would become renowned for throwing grand scale parties in their Queen Square home and attending the society functions of the day.

Though this heady existence was far out of reach of the average Bristolian, Sarah Guppy had a fierce intellect and it seems that a life based solely on socialising could not satisfy her inquisitive mind, so Sarah began working on designs and inventions, patenting her first in 1811.

The patent was for bridge foundations that could reliably stand in water. Her method was to bind pillars together so that the ebb and flow of water would not rip them apart. This design worked precisely as she'd hoped and was utilised on many bridges at the time - not least by Thomas Telford.

That Guppy designed a bridge to go over the Avon Gorge - and because Thomas Telford's design for his Clifton Suspension Bridge relied on her foundation patent, are likely what has led to a long-standing rumour that Sarah Guppy was the true inventor of the Clifton Suspension Bridge.

Brunel was friends with both Sarah and Samuel Guppy, but his bridge design did not rely on Sarah's invention at all, as its foundations are embedded in the gorge itself, rather than the river below.

Sarah Guppy did assist Brunel with parts of the Great Western Railway, and her idea of planting trees and shrubs along steep embankments to prevent erosion is still used by GWR today.

Among some of her patents were more domestic inventions, including a contraption for boiling eggs at speed and even a bed which could transform into exercise equipment (which may sound faintly ridiculous today, but the Georgians enjoyed nothing more than exercise fads).

For a long time it's been hard to fully establish which inventions had been devised by Sarah and which her husband had created, as the patents were usually submitted under their family name, but it's now believed that a method for removing and preventing the growth of barnacles on ships' undersides was probably conceived by Sarah but patented under her husband's name.

Samuel died in 1830 and she went on to scandalise Bristol society by marrying a man 28 years' her junior. Richard Eyre Coote appears to have been something of a poor choice for Sarah, as he did little more than waste her money on drink and gambling. A few years later the couple separated and she purchased 7 Richmond Hill, and the plot of land opposite, which she offered the use of to the people of Clifton. She would live here until her death in 1852, aged 82.

Sarah Guppy doesn't seem to get the amount of recognition she deserves. As a woman of her time, she defied all expectations and excelled in a field which is, to this day, still predominately male. Perhaps this is how she would have preferred it, as when asked why she had not sought greater recognition for her achievements, her response was somehow both humble yet tragic: "It is unpleasant to speak of oneself - it may seem boastful, particularly in a woman."

*From one pioneering woman to several more. Our next destination can be found by walking the remaining length of Richmond Hill and then turning left. The Victoria Rooms cannot be missed as it's the large building on the roundabout with a set of grand fountains in front of it.*

## 10. The Bristol Suffragettes

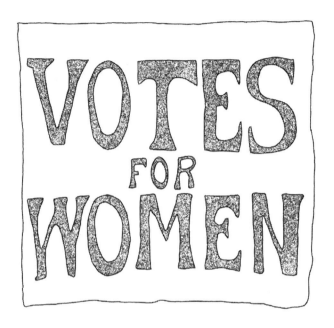

The grand building at the roundabout which connects Park Street and Whiteladies Road, most notable for its elaborate Art Nouveau fountains, is often referred to as the Assembly Rooms, but is officially known as the Victoria Rooms. Opened in 1842, they were at the centre of high society in the area.

The building is remembered for having hosted not just elaborate parties for the elite of Clifton throughout the Victorian era, but also readings by Charles Dickens and a performance by Jenny Lind "The Swedish Nightingale". In the 1890s it also became the base for the Bristol suffragette movement.

Bristol had the largest, and most active, suffragette group outside of London and their meetings were held in the Victoria Rooms once a month. This was quite a scandal at the time as the suffragettes (who met under the name of The Women's Social and Political Union) were seen not just as politically radical, but also prone to militant acts of vandalism - unlike the more law abiding suffragists of the time. In fact, it was so notorious at one point the group employed boxers to work as security on the doors of the building.

One of the most notable leaders of the WSPU was Annie Kenney, who is best remembered as one of the most powerful voices in the movement - and also for being among the very few working-class women to make it into the higher ranks of the organisation.

Kenney possibly popularised the term "deeds not words" among the Bristol suffragettes, and openly called for the women of Bristol to break the law in pursuit of justice. She was also extremely well connected to the Pankhurst family (probably even having a long relationship with Christabel Pankhurst, daughter of the movement's founder, Emmeline) making the Bristol suffragettes among the most dedicated and well-organised.

Among dozens of acts of civil disobedience, some of the most memorable activities by the Bristol WSJU included the time in 1909 when Elsie Howey and Vera Holme hid overnight in the Colston Hall organ so that they could disrupt a speech by notorious anti-women's suffrage politician Augustine Birrell with shouts of "Votes for women!"

In 1913, a group of women burned down Begbrook House, near Frenchay. The house belonged to a wealthy banker (though it had been empty for many years) and was destroyed in protest against the force-feeding of suffragettes on hunger strike in prison.

Perhaps the most audacious event of all happened in 1912. When Winston Churchill, known for his staunch opposition to women's votes, visited Bristol to give a speech on the topic - he was met at Temple Meads by Theresa Garnett who attempted to attack the MP with a horse whip.

She was sent to Horfield Prison for several months, and while there went on hunger strike and set fire to her own cell in protest at the injustice.

The militant actions of the suffragettes, and whether or not they helped or hindered the fight for women's suffrage, are still argued today, but it should never be forgotten that these women felt they had no other option - if the nation would not allow them to have their voices heard, they would just have to force it to listen to them.

*That concludes our tour of Clifton. The next walk, which is a mixed bag of oddities concerning Park Street and the surrounding area, begins down the hill from the Victoria Rooms, and the Triangle. The building you are looking for is the Bristol Museum and Art Gallery, which will be on the left. If it's open, go inside and follow the signs to "Alfred the Gorilla".*

# Walk Seven
## Beyond Park Street

# Beyond Park Street

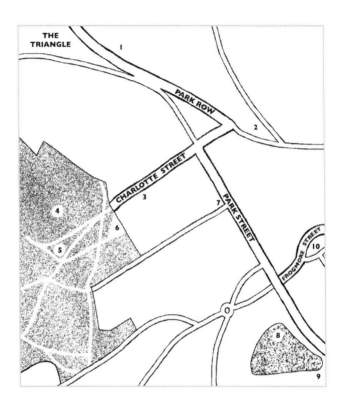

Often credited with inspiring newcomers' love of the city, Park Street is one of our most popular locations. The beautiful architecture and relaxing green spaces have been a fixture of the city for as long as anyone can remember and its location, running through some of Bristol's most fascinating areas, has ensured that a good deal of weird history can be found right here.

On this walk we have a bit of a concentration on crime. There's an audacious heist of a gorilla from Bristol Museum, an almost forgotten wartime protest which turned into a bloody riot, and a pair of hair-raising murders which shocked the nation. But fear not, there are a few light-hearted stops along the way too!

## 1. The Gorilla Heist

On an autumn morning in 1956, workers at Bristol Museum arrived to discover that the taxidermied body of Alfred the Gorilla, one of the city's most beloved former residents, had vanished, presumed stolen.

Three days later, Alfred was found intact in one of the University of Bristol's common rooms. The culprits would not be found for over fifty years.

Alfred the Gorilla had been a star attraction for Bristol Zoo, but during WWII he became something far more important - a sort of emblem for the city.

Born in what was then the Belgian Congo in 1928, the story of his discovery as a baby is that he was rescued by American members of an expedition after both of his parents had been shot.

The veracity of this story (which very conveniently makes the Americans who profited from Alfred's sale completely innocent of his parents' deaths) has been called into question many times, but what is known is that the baby gorilla was shipped around the world to several locations before he was sold to Bristol Zoo in 1930.

He was an instant sensation with the visitors, especially children. The western lowland gorilla had a strange sort of rapport with people and though he could be belligerent, sometimes even aggressively so, for the most part he seemed to be at ease with the presence of humans.

For many visitors, looking into his eyes was the first time they had ever seen an animal which had that spark of intelligence - that humanity possessed by all great apes - and the experience was both unnerving and profound.

It was during the Second World War that Alfred became internationally recognised. While US troops were stationed in Bristol, Alfred became a draw for them too and he enchanted his American visitors by pulling strange faces and throwing snowballs at them in the winter. He became the subject of a series of postcards which troops were soon sending home to their families overseas, and with them, Alfred's fame spread.

For the people of Bristol during this time, Alfred's sheer size and power, the resilience and bravery he had shown during the city's air raids, as well as his mischievous nature, all came to symbolise the character of Bristol during this terrible time. He was adopted, in a way, as an emblem for the city itself.

When he died in 1948, a great deal of grief was felt across Bristol, a lot of people weren't even entirely sure why they had been so moved by the death of this captive animal, besides the fact that he had meant *something* to them during Bristol's darkest days.

News of his death was reported as far away as American and China and there were calls for the animal to be given a full funeral service. This was not to be, as his organs were sent to the university, for dissection, and the rest was taxidermied before going on display in the museum.

The mystery around his disappearance was only solved in 2010, following the death of Ron Morgan, aged 79. His family came forward with images of Alfred along with three students from the University of Bristol.

His kidnapping had been little more than a youthful prank to coincide with "rag week" - an annual event consisting of mischief-making at the university. Morgan, along with his friend Fred Hooper and a further accomplice who still remains anonymous, snuck into the museum after hours by using a door which connected it to the adjacent student building.

They had not been prepared for the outpouring of shock and anger across the city and the three young men began to panic. With tightened security at the museum, they had no choice but to place him in one of the common rooms and hope for the best. They decided that their ill-advised prank had caused more trouble than it was worth and the trio of kidnappers decided to take the secret to their graves.

*Follow Park Street down from the museum and when it forks, take the left side onto Park Row and continue on until you find a large building, belonging to the Society of Merchant Venturers. It is situated across from a petrol station. Over the entrance to the building there is a small statue of a dog. His name is Nipper and he is the subject of the next stop on the tour.*

## 2. Nipper: Bristol's Most Famous Dog

At the top of Park Row, near to the intersection where it joins Park Street, there is a large, sandstone building that sits opposite the road to a petrol station. If you look above one of the entrances (on the side next to a Victorian toilet block) you will see a charming little statue of a dog - this is a memorial to Nipper - Bristol's most famous canine.

The statue was installed in 2000 and is thought to be roughly life sized to the real Nipper, who was born in Bristol in 1884. His breed is something of a mystery but he is generally thought to be a terrier mix of some sort.

Nipper originally lived with his owner Mark Henry Barraud in the Princes Theatre, where a garage now stands (this theatre was one of the victims of the Bristol Blitz). Barraud was a scenery designer who rented a small room in the theatre's roof space. Nipper was like a shadow to his master, following him wherever he went and protecting him from any perceived threat (his name came from his tendency to nip at the heels of strangers who approached his master.)

In 1887 Barraud died quite unexpectedly and poor Nipper was sent to live with his master's brother, Francis Barraud, who was an artist living in London.

Francis Barraud was an accomplished painter, known particularly for his realistic animals. Inevitably, Nipper became the subject of a delightful piece in which the dog was seen staring into the horn of a gramophone, as if listening to the recording.

It was a hugely popular image and was often exhibited with the (probably untrue) story that Nipper was forlornly listening to a recording of his deceased master's voice.

167

In 1899, Francis sold the rights to the painting, now named *"His Master's Voice"* to The Victor Talking Machine Company, which specialised in making wax cylinder recordings. The company later renamed itself after the painting - which had become one of the most famous advertising logos in the world, and later still, went by the name HMV.

It's believed that Francis' painting of Nipper may be the most reproduced and well-known image of a dog in the history of the world, and remains the logo of the company to this day.

Nipper died in 1895 - before the painting was even completed. He could not have had any idea just how far and wide his likeness would spread, but in Bristol this humble reproduction of a tenacious little dog is our way of memorialising another of Bristol's most unlikely heroes.

*Walk back a little along Park Row and take the first left, Park Street Avenue, until it joins Park Street. Charlotte Street is directly across the road. The property we are looking for no longer exists, but it was found on the left side of the street when looking uphill, and was situated about halfway along.*

## 3. The Birth of a Design Classic

Charlotte Street, just off of Park Street may not seem like the kind of place you'd expect to find the origin of one of the most popular and enduring icons of modern design, but in 1926, this street birthed a legend.

It was the year in which Douglas Cleverdon, the proprietor of a bookshop which stood on the spot of 18 Charlotte Street asked his friend, Eric Gill, who was a noted artist, to design him a bold and eye-catching sign for his shop.

Gill did just that and the resulting sign would be the first ever use of the typeface which would come to be known as Gill Sans.

The sign was so striking that it was soon being discussed among design enthusiasts and the shop was visited by Stanley Morison, the typographer who would go on to design Times New Roman - another of the 20th century's most influential typefaces. He commissioned Gill to design an entire font set in the style.

Gill Sans was based on Johnston, a sans-serif typeface designed by Edward Johnston in 1916, which is best known for being the official font of the London Underground. Gill had worked with Johnston and had no qualms about admitting his influence, but Gill Sans was often seen as the more appealing and less corporate of the two.

The popularity of Gill Sans was also due, in part, to the fact that Johnston remained the legal property of the London Passenger Transport Board who would not allow it for public use.

Eric Gill remained a popular artist and designer throughout his life, and for many years after his death, aged 58 in 1940, he was spoken of with reverence.

His reputation would be irreparably destroyed several decades later when his private diaries were exposed. In them he had documented a litany of horror and perversion, including incest, paedophilia and bestiality.

Unsurprisingly, this led to a major reassessment of his work and he continues to be a divisive figure among design enthusiasts, as well as being a near casebook example of whether it's possible to separate art from its artist.

The story of Eric Gill is so at odds with his arresting creations - his most famous of which was born on this Bristol street, but perhaps it is an important thing to remember that even the ugliest, most depraved minds are somehow still capable of creating beauty.

*Continue uphill on Charlotte Street until you reach Brandon Hill. Any and all of the paths here will reveal Cabot Tower in all its glory. I recommend climbing it to the top if you can, otherwise, anywhere with it in view will suffice.*

## 4. Cabot Tower

Towering over Brandon Hill, and visible for miles around as one of the most recognisable points of the Bristol skyline, is Cabot Tower.

Built to celebrate the 400th anniversary of John Cabot's 1497 voyage to the New World, where he became the first European to set foot on continental America, the project was completed a little late and opened in 1898. The same year, work began on another Cabot Tower, marking the supposed end point of his journey in Newfoundland. It was completed in 1900.

It stands at 105 ft tall over the already high Brandon Hill and the topmost viewing point is one of the highest public spaces in the city. It's so high, that if you were to walk from College Green, up Brandon Hill and to the top of the tower one hundred times, you would have climbed the equivalent height of Mount Everest.

One of the lesser-known reasons for its construction can be found inscribed in a series of plaques around the base. It was hoped that this tower would be a permanent symbol of the friendship between Britain and the United States of America.

Since 1776 and the American War of Independence (and the 1812 "rematch" which Britain also lost) relations between the two nations had been rather shaky throughout much of the 19th century, but during the Victorian era, a sort of friendly alliance had arisen, thanks largely to trade deals.

Gestures such as this tower, meant to enforce this "special relationship," were not uncommon in Britain at the time and Bristol's 400th year celebrations of the voyage of the Matthew were seen as good a time as any to help foster that still-burgeoning alliance. In a way it can be seen as much as a symbol of friendship as a celebration of discovery.

The tower also transmits a secret code across the city every night. As worrying as that may sound, in my intentionally alarmist wording, it's nothing more than a rather friendly morse code light which, after fourteen years of repairs, is now up and running again.

It's often mistakenly assumed that this signal is the red light that can be seen at night, but this is nothing more than a warning light to low flying planes, which flashes at a constant rate. The actual light you should look for is a bit smaller and white and has an erratic pattern.

So what is it saying? Well, most of the time it's nothing more than "B-R-I-S-T-O-L" but for special occasions, it's sometimes programmed to signal other things, most notably throughout Advent when it messages "M-E-R-R-Y C-H-R-I-S-M-A-S" and "G-O-D S-A-V-E T-H-E Q-U-E-E-N" on her Majesty's 90th birthday.

Perhaps most touching of all was on the night before the 1997 built replica of Cabot's ship The Matthew was due to leave Bristol and retrace his voyage for the 500th anniversary, Cabot Tower, overlooking the perilously small ship in the harbour, offered "G-O-D-S-P-E-E-D M-A-T-T-H-E-W".

*At the foot of the landscaped mound upon which Cabot Tower stands, there is a magnificent view over the harbour. This will be the location for our next stop.*

## 5. The Gatecrashers of the Reform Party

The 1831 Queen Square riots had been among the most violent the city had ever experienced (there is a chapter dedicated to them on the next tour, through King Street and Queen Square). Though many factors contributed to this sudden outburst of protest, the most pressing was how few people were permitted to vote.

With much of the Square still in ruins, plans were quickly drawn up to enfranchise more of the men of the city and the result was a Reform Act which allowed an additional 4,000 people the right to take part in local elections.

On the surface, this may sound like a step in the right direction, but upon closer inspection, this made the situation even worse. All the men included in the Reform Act were wealthy and middle class, and none of them were regarded as the kind of people who would seek radical change for the city - or be interested in the plight of the poor.

Nevertheless, plans for a huge celebration were put in place, culminating in a huge banquet on Brandon Hill, to which 6,000 people would be invited. It was to be a lavish affair, with copious food and alcohol consumed in the August air from noon until night.

At first, everything seemed to be going well. The guests arrived and soon Brandon Hill was buzzing with the elite of the city, drinking wine and listening to a band play music. A few rabble-rousers had arrived and were demanding entry to the city's oldest public park, but a security cordon, lined with police officers, ensured none of them were allowed in.

However, as the day wore on, more and more uninvited guests were appearing, and they were getting angry. The contrast of the idle rich and the working poor the banquet represented had fanned the flames of another Bristol uprising and by mid-afternoon a crowd of over 14,000 people had gathered around the hill.

At this point, the cordon was of no use and the gate-crashers simply rushed Brandon Hill in huge numbers. The party was immediately transformed into a scene of mayhem.

People were dancing on tables, men were parading around the park wearing women's hats they'd stolen and fine wine was being glugged from bottles.

Fights were soon breaking out, and at one point, a gang of men managed to successfully roll barrels of beer down the hill into the working class district below.

The havoc continued well into the night, by which time all the alcohol had gone and the gatecrashers had either decided their point had been proven or were too drunk to continue revelling.

One man had been stabbed, but made a full recovery. Brandon Hill was a scene of chaos, with upturned tables and drunk people scattered everywhere.

While this somewhat comical show of strength between the disenfranchised people of the city may have been justifiable, at the time it was argued that this was exactly why the working class should not be permitted to vote - as they had proved themselves to be little more than hooligans with no respect for their social superiors!

*Surrounding most of Brandon Hill is a high stone wall. Head back towards Charlotte Street, where a section of this wall can be found. It hides a rather creepy secret which will be the subject of our next stop.*

## 6. The Spiders of Brandon Hill

The next time you find yourself on Brandon Hill, look closely at the wall which runs the perimeter of this beautiful park, just off Park Street (featuring some of the most breathtakingly picturesque views of the city). In this wall, there lives a venomous invader...

Look closer still if you dare and you may spot spokes of webbing emerging from little holes along the wall. Look even closer and you will see that the spokes intertwine to form a funnel - a web in which one of our city's strangest inhabitants may be found hiding.

These are segestria florentina - or the tube web spider. It is the largest of the segestriid spiders, which means it has only six eyes, compared to most spiders, which have eight. They're found all over Europe, particularly the Mediterranean, but are not native to Britain. Bristol has been home to huge numbers of them for hundreds of years, and this wall on Brandon Hill seems to be their favourite place.

It's believed that they first came to Bristol in the late 18th century. The period was a heyday for the city as an international port, with ships arriving from foreign destinations every day.

Back then, ships would often make seed or grass ballasts - soft sacks of organic matter which were hung over the side of vessels to ensure balance and to minimise damage when coming into dock. Because of the nature of international trade, ships would make these ballasts with whatever plants they had to hand, and could accidentally introduce foreign species to ecosystems that may not have been able to handle them.

So many ships coming into Bristol used these ballasts, that all along the route of the River Avon from the Bristol Channel, you can find rare and exotic plants from all over the world, the descendants of those carried here as seeds on ships. This is how it's thought that the tube web spiders came to Bristol and they have been breeding here ever since.

Now, I don't wish to alarm any arachnophobes reading this, but these spiders are venomous, and their bite is said to be really quite painful, but I haven't been able to find a record of anyone having been bitten by one of these shy and solitary creatures in over a century, and there have never been cases of the venom being fatal to humans. If you leave them alone, they'll do the same to you.

Bristol isn't the only place in Britain to have a population of these spiders. They can be found in a handful of other port cities, and the seed ballasts seem to have made their way to Bath and Bradford on Avon too, as colonies of them can be found there. They're actually quite beautiful little creatures with vivid green markings - but as is so often the case with nature, these spiders should be admired only from a distance…

*Follow Charlotte Street back to Park Street and then head downhill until you reach where it meets Great George Street on the right. This corner is the next destination.*

## 7. The Park Street Riot

Despite its huge scale, the ferocity of the fighting and its relative recency in history, the Park Street riot of 1944 has almost been completely forgotten. Perhaps it's because it wasn't between Bristolians, or even British people, or perhaps it's because of the horrible implications of Bristol's complicity in racial segregation.

During WWII, Park Street saw more than its fair share of bombing. The worst night of the Bristol Blitz, the 24th of November 1940, over 30 buildings along the street were completely destroyed whilst many others, including the Bristol Museum, were severely damaged. Most of these were rebuilt according to their original plans and are now almost indistinguishable from the pre-existing buildings.

In the later years of the war, long after the blitz had finished, Park Street was significant for American involvement as many US soldiers were stationed around here, most notably, on Great George Street and the Victoria Rooms, both of which acted as social clubs for American troops.

However, the US army was strictly segregated at this time and one of the conditions of their stay in Britain was that the cities which hosted them would keep white and non-white (mostly black) soldiers completely segregated.

When Eleanor Roosevelt visited Bristol in 1944, her itinerary included visits to both the "Whites" and "Coloreds" social clubs, with the latter being on Great George Street.

That Bristol followed these orders is disappointing but not a surprise, as by this time the country needed any help it could get. However, it's heartening to read that many of the black soldiers found Bristolians very

177

accommodating, with Ben Greer, the father of US author Bonnie Greer, describing his stint in Bristol as being the "first decent experience of white people I'd ever had." - If you can track down her terrific documentary on black soldiers in Bristol during WWII, I highly recommend it.

Not all of the experiences were positive though, and there were incidences of fights, particularly in pubs, but it took one such pub to break the segregation rules for a domino effect to spread across Bristol. The Colston Arms on St Michael's Hill was the first to defy the racial bar and allow both black and white soldiers to be served, and soon, most of the businesses across the city followed suit.

Despite this, Park Street itself had been designated as "whites only" - not just the businesses along it, but the street itself was only accessible to white American soldiers in order to ensure there was no fraternising of races between the social clubs.

Understandably this caused a huge amount of anger, and on the evening of the 15th of July 1944 several dozen black and minority ethnic soldiers marched on Park Street in an act of defiance.

Soon a huge fight broke out, with over 400 soldiers involved and, after more than an hour, over 100 military police were sent in to try and break it up.

This seems to have only stoked the flames and soon weapons were drawn. Several soldiers were shot by the police, resulting in one fatality. A military police officer was also stabbed but recovered soon afterwards. The violence resulted in all American soldiers being put under strict curfew for several nights.

That night on Park Street should never be forgotten, not just for the bloodshed that occurred, but as a reminder of the evils of segregation.

*We're onto happier times next - and what's happier than uni-corns? Head down Park Street until you reach College Green. On top of the City Hall building on your right are two magnificent specimens which will be the subject of our next stop.*

# 8. The Mystery of the Unicorns

The two unicorns which stand proudly atop City Hall (usually called the Council Building) are among the most evocative symbols of the city. Instantly recognisable and beloved for generations, the story of how they came to be here was, for some time, a mystery.

Bristol has had a long history with unicorns. Two of them appear on the city's 1569 crest as emblems of virtue, while a unicorn head, carved in wood and dating back to the 14th century can be found in Bristol Cathedral. It's not known quite when this association was made but once you start looking for them, you will start seeing unicorns all over the city!

City Hall was built in 1950 and proved to be immediately popular. Very few buildings constructed in the post war years had much architectural beauty, but the council building - designed as a pastiche of ancient Roman style, was an instant hit.

There was just one thing wrong. The 600 ft long ornamental iron ridging which was intended to run the length of the roof had never materialised - despite being part of the original design. The architect of the building, Vincent Harris, had claimed that there was a holdup at the manufacturing stage, so Bristol would have to wait a while longer for the building to be finished.

What eventually arrived were two large, highly stylised gold leaf unicorns. This caused an enormous amount of confusion to the council as they had never been part of the original blueprint - and on top of that, nobody was able to contact Harris as he had gone away to Italy on holiday.

When he returned, the full story was revealed. He had never liked the iron edging on the roof and found it an ugly waste of money, but felt the building still needed something to feel "finished" so instead spent the money on commissioning a pair of unicorns.

The unicorns are rather peculiar things, modelled more like deer than horses and with unreasonably long horns, but when a photograph of them was published in the local newspapers, the public all but unanimously agreed that the unicorns just *felt* like they belonged on top of the building.

In October 1950 a crowd gathered to watch the two figures be hoisted to the roof and a cheer was heard as they were fixed into place.

Gleaming atop City Hall they have stood ever since and are frequently counted among the finest public sculptures in Bristol. Vincent Harris' secret gift to the city will continue to delight and charm for generations.

*With your back to City Hall, work your way across College Green until you reach the statue of Queen Victoria outside the Marriott hotel for our next stop on the tour.*

## 9. The Goodere Murder

The 1888 statue of Queen Victoria outside the Marriott on College Green is one of the most austere in the city, surveying Bristol with a dour, even hostile expression, but where she now stands was, in 1741, home to a solicitor's office which became embroiled in one of the most sensational murders in British history.

At this point in time Bristol was one of the most important shipping ports in the world but Park Street was little more than a dirt track with farmland on either side and College Green just a scattering of houses close to the cathedral.

Living nearby were two brothers, Sir John and Samuel Goodere. Both in their mid-twenties, Sir John was the older of the brothers and was the only one to have inherited a title. The two young men appear to have had a problematic relationship, and it was claimed that Samuel was jealous of his older brother, not just for his title, but for having married into a very wealthy family and living a life of leisure, while he had to work as a captain of a naval ship named HMS Ruby.

In October of 1740, Sir John made the fatal decision to write his brother out of his will after a particularly brutal argument and it seems it was at this point that Samuel made his decision - although he would inherit no money from his brother's death, he would murder him purely out of hatred.

On the 13th of January the following year, Samuel arranged to meet Sir John at a solicitor's office on what is now College Green and the two brothers were witnessed reconciling and toasting to "brotherly love and friendship." This was part of Samuel's ruse, believing that as the men had been seen acting amicably, suspicion for Sir John's murder would never fall on him.

It was as they were leaving that Sir John became aware of the subterfuge. In the early evening, as he turned to walk down the hill towards the quay, a gang of vagrants - who'd been paid by Samuel - seized him and dragged him to the docks in full view of dozens of people.

Why nobody intervened when Sir John pleaded for help is probably due to the nature of the docks themselves. They were often a dangerous place with drunken fights an everyday occurrence, plus the loathed privateers were in the habit of forcing unemployed men to work on their ships, so most people were in the habit of not interfering in even the most troubling confrontations around the harbour.

Sir John was bundled onto HMS Ruby, which was then sailed from the city and moored in the River Avon. Onboard were his brother, a petty criminal named Matthew Mahoney, who'd helped Samuel Goodere form a gang to kidnap Sir John, and a handful of sailors, many of whom had no idea of what was going on.

Sir John was locked into the purser's cabin and after imbibing a huge amount of rum, Charles White, one of the sailors - who'd been told that Sir John was actually a Spaniard who had come to Bristol to plan an invasion - was tasked with strangling him. The strangulation was such a gruesome affair that it woke many of the sailors, some of whom witnessed the murder through cracks in the ships panelling.

Two of these sailors took to a small boat and rowed back to Bristol, where they informed the police of all they had seen. When HMS Ruby returned to Bristol a few hours later, everyone onboard was arrested.

The trial was a media sensation and was spoken of across the country. The brothers' high social standing and links to the aristocracy, alongside the brutal slaying, were the perfect ingredients for the nation's love of morbid horror and the trial, commencing early in March, was reported daily.

Samuel Goodere, Matthew Mahoney and Charles White were all found guilty of murder and within a week all of them had been hanged.

Samuel's body was left in a gibbet to swing over the street for several weeks as a warning to others, that no matter how noble your lineage, justice is blind to all but the truth...

*One more stop on our tour - and it's another gruesome one. We are heading for the Hatchet, which is a pub on Frogmore Street. At the City Hall end of College Green, cross Park Street and head down the steps which lead under the bridge (where Banksy's "Well-Hung Man" mural can be seen). The Hatchet is a large, Tudor building surrounded by roads on all sides. Head to the front door.*

## 10. The Skin Door

One of the most oft-repeated - and grisly - legends of Bristol concerns the Hatchet Inn.

First licensed in 1606, it was probably operating even earlier than that and its claim to be the oldest pub in Bristol is quite possibly true. It now enjoys a reputation as a somewhat counterculture music venue with an eclectic mix of patrons at the weekend.

The door to the pub is estimated to be at least 300 years old and it's rumoured that, under the layers of paint, it is lined with the skins of executed criminals...

Could this possibly be true? What tests have been carried out on it have been either negative or inconclusive for traces of human skin, but the story was convincing enough for an American tourist in the 1960s to offer an enormous sum of money to buy it as a morbid trophy. The offer was declined.

Further tales suggested that the walls of the pub itself were lined with more human skin but this seems little more than an embellishment of the original tale. However, it's not inconceivable that skin could have been used in this manner at some point, as the city has had a rather macabre history with such things...

We have in Bristol one of the few verified examples of what is called anthropodermic bibliopegy - binding books in human skin. The book can be seen in The M Shed Museum where it's a queasy reminder of the horrors of the past.

The skin belonged to John Horwood, a man in his early twenties who was accused of murdering Eliza Balsom, a woman he had become somewhat obsessed with, and who had continually declined his invitations to marriage.

Nowadays, we'd likely understand Horwood as being a vulnerable person with learning difficulties, but back in 1821, this was no barrier to him being afforded a public trial.

He had seen Eliza walking with another man on the afternoon of the 25th of January and had thrown a stone at her. It had hit her in the temple and knocked her unconscious. She was rushed to hospital where a doctor tried a radical - and untested - operation to relieve what he considered was a dangerous blood clot in her brain.

She died during the operation. It's now believed that it may have been the doctor's attempts to save Balsom with experimental surgery (including trepanning, which required drilling into her skull) which actually killed her.

Nevertheless, Horwood was found guilty and hanged. His skin was stripped from his body and leathered in animal urine and his trial notes were bound in it. The remains of his body were sent to the University of Bristol for dissection. His skeleton, still with a noose around its neck, remained in an office cupboard until it was buried in 2012.

So it is possible that the Hatchet's gruesome claim to fame is true. The reason for this morbid desecration of human bodies was meant to be a secondary deterrent to would-be criminals as, it was believed by some, that without an intact body you could not be resurrected on Judgement Day.

Whatever the truth behind the Hatchet's door, the story will continue - and countless people will shudder as they pass it, for many years to come.

*That concludes our wander around Park Street. If you're looking for some more dark history, I recommend the next walk, which has quite a ghostly theme and will take you through King Street and Queen Square. To reach the start of the next walk, cross St Augustine's Parade and head for the corner of Kings Street where the Merchant Venturer's almshouses can be found behind railings.*

# Walk Eight

## King Street

### & Queen Square

# King Street and Queen Square

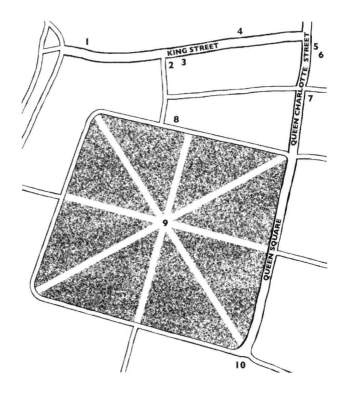

King Street may be one of the most beautiful and ancient in Bristol, but this walk along its cobbles to the equally picturesque Queen Square may be the bloodiest in the book.

As charming as this area may be, don't be fooled into thinking that its history will be equally as quaint. There's a definite darkness to this walk, which will recount some of the city's spookiest ghost stories as well as tales of pirates and privateers, a statue which depicts the moment a king was fatally injured and one of the most devastating riots in the history of the city.

# 1. The Merchant Venturer's Almshouses

The unmistakable pink building to the west of Kings Street is a charming little haven in the city centre, with pretty gardens and a kind of bucolic tranquility that feels almost out of place in a contemporary city.

These are the Merchant Venturers Almshouses and were built sometime around 1696. It was about this time that many of the wealthiest people of Bristol began funding these housing complexes, which were charitable establishments intended to home deprived or neglected people.

Another set of almshouses can be found at the opposite end of Kings Street. The St Nicholas Almshouses have a distinct Dutch style, inspired by the merchants from the Netherlands who had contributed money to their 1656 construction.

The Foster's Almshouses were established in 1492 but the current, almost fairytale-esque building which now stands at the junction of Colston Street and Christmas Steps was built in 1883.

On St Michael's Hill you can find the Colston Almshouses, named after their investor Edward Colston. The roof rafters of the chapel on the grounds were made from timber salvaged from Colston's own ships - some of which were likely used to transport slaves.

The Merchant Venturers Almshouses were built to house sailors who were involved in the slave trade, so they could enjoy a secure retirement. The eye-raising dedication to them on the front of the building poetically describes their heroic trials upon the sea in a manner which sits quite uncomfortably with many modern-day attitudes but serves as an important reminder of prevailing opinions at the time.

The Society of Merchant Venturers, who were the financial backers of these almshouses have, for a long, long time, been part of Bristol's culture - both good and bad. Founded initially as a guild of tradesmen in the 13th century, the current society was officially established in 1552 as a collective of wealthy merchants and tradesmen from across the city.

Over the centuries they have been the power behind a lot of the large-scale developments in Bristol, from the Clifton Suspension Bridge to the Floating Harbour. It's hard to find any significant changes to the city that they didn't play a role in.

The Society still exists today and continues to be the subject of controversy and conspiracy theory. Their links to the city's slave trading history is a frequent source of criticism, as is their membership - which only voted to allow women to join in 2003.

The society owned a building next to the almshouses, which served as their meeting house until it was destroyed in the blitz. The almshouses themselves survived the bombing but were the victims of town planning. The gardens you see now were once fully enclosed courtyards, with a fourth side, containing more homes, sealing them off from the public. The fourth side was later knocked down to allow for road widening.

On the wall of an adjoining building, you can see the crest belonging to the Society of Merchant Venturers. Upon it are a mermaid and a satyr, along with the group's motto: *Indocillus pauperiem pati* - "We shall not learn to endure poverty."

*It's a quick skip to the next stop, the King William Pub further down King Street. It is an orange building on the opposite side of the road to the almshouses.*

## 2. The King William Pub

The King William Pub on King Street, was built in 1670 and along with its two adjoining neighbours, was part of a complex built to house poor women and widows who would otherwise have been homeless.

It's not known why or exactly when these almshouses were turned into taverns, but the King William seems to have been the first to have done so.

Throughout its long history it has been a popular draw for sailors and merchants and, during the construction of the SS Great Britain, was apparently the pub of choice for builders and foremen of the project.

It is named in honour of King William III - a statue of whom can be found in King's Square (more on the statue can be found later on in this walk). William III is known to have visited the city only once, in 1690 when he moored at the mouth of the River Avon and arrived in the city on horseback. His ship was too large to navigate the river.

His stay in Bristol was incredibly brief - a matter of mere hours, but was seen as significant enough for a pub to be named in his honour and for the statue to be erected (both following his death).

Not all of the pub's history appears to have stayed in the past, as it's said to be home to one of the city's creepiest ghosts.

The rear staircase of the King William has been the subject of a supposed haunting for decades. The ghost is rarely seen but manifests itself as cold spots, where the temperature feels significantly lower than the surrounding area.

The ghost has also been accused of walking heavily up and down the same staircase and perhaps most menacingly, shouting the names of bar staff from the land-ing.

On the few times the ghost has been reported to have been seen, he has been described as a middle-aged man. One witness to his appearance later swore the man was none other than Captain John Gray - the captain of the SS Great Britain who disappeared while at sea in 1872 and is thought to have died by suicide.

Gray's ghost is also said to haunt the ship itself, and it is believed that he may well have been a regular at the King William while it was being built.

*There's no need to wander far along here but look for the strips of dark metal which run the length of the pavements. They will be the subject of our next stop.*

## 3. The Pavement Edgings

Sir John Betjeman once said that in order for us to truly understand a city, one had simply to "look up". He was, of course, correct. So often we go about our daily lives without noticing the history which is all around us, but I would add that sometimes it's good to look down too - otherwise you might miss this curio from Bristol's past.

The iron edging which runs the length of the pavements can be found all over the city, but it's in abundance along King Street. Initially it would have been a silvery-grey colour but exposure to the elements has turned it a deep brown.

It was installed as an experiment ahead of being rolled out in towns and cities across the world and was supposed to be a solution to a problem many urban centres were struggling with - wear to the edges of pavements caused by the wheels of carts and wagons.

For a long time, this hadn't been much of an issue. The wooden wheels of vehicles were soft enough that they couldn't do major damage to the stonework but by the 1880s, most wheels had a metal ridge running around them to prevent frequent replacements, and these were proving to be very damaging to pavements.

Bristol, Leeds and Southampton were all selected as places to trial iron edging, which was hoped would prevent further erosion - and while it's hard to ascertain why these three places in particular were chosen, Bristol was the only one to extensively use it across their streets.

It was a complete success and between the 1890s and early 1920s, more and more of it was installed. Sections can still be seen in parts of Bristol as far away as Bedminster and Redland.

Plans were stopped before it had been installed all across the city. The edging was expensive, but not so much as the maintenance that otherwise needed to be done to the roads. It stopped because by the 1920s, it was apparent that the vehicle of choice for the 20th century would be the motorcar.

Though it's a shame the project was never completed - as it has meant that many of our ancient streets have remained remarkably intact, it is one of those charming mementos of the past that let us peek through time to see how our city would once have been.

*Another short hop across the road. We're going to the Bristol Old Vic!*

## 4. The Bristol Old Vic

The Bristol Old Vic has many claims to fame, not least of all the incredible roster of talent which has passed through its doors - both in its school and its performance company but its antiquity has played an equal role in its international reputation.

Opening its doors for the very first time in 1766, it predates all surviving British repertory theatres and is by some margin, the oldest continually operating theatre in the English speaking world.

In 2016, when the Old Vic marked its 250th anniversary with a season of performances from some of its most celebrated alumni, it became the first theatre in the world known to have celebrated that milestone.

The interior of the theatre is renowned as being among the finest in the world, but a unique installation in the building's rafters is a lesser-known gem to be found inside.

Known as a thunder run, it is a series of channels through which cannonballs can be rolled. The motion on the wood creates the uncanny sound of thunder, which is capable of being heard throughout the theatre.

Before 2016, the thunder run hadn't been used since 1942, but as part of the restoration works to coincide with the 250th anniversary, the contraption was put back to working order and was used as part of that season's production of King Lear, starring Tim West.

An old theatre couldn't really be a theatre without a ghost - and one as ancient as the Old Vic should be entitled to at least two - which is has - and possibly more, if rumours are to be believed.

The two ghosts most commonly recognised as being visitors to the theatre are both women and both called Sarah.

One of them is supposedly the ghost of Sarah Siddons, the legendary Georgian actor, who also seems to spend some of her time in the nearby Llandoger Trow. The other is believed to be the former manager of the theatre, Sarah Macready.

From 1829, Macready took control of the theatre and was said to do so with a ferocious authority. It was said that she was not the kind of woman one would like to be on the wrong side of, but her no-nonsense approach to dealing with actors' demands won her much admiration.

Appearances of the ghost of Sarah Macready are said to be preceded by the smell of lavender and she is often spotted near the box office where she used to keep a watchful eye over the audience as they arrived.

Perhaps even more mysteriously, during maintenance work in the 1980s, a human skeleton was discovered in the basement and in the 1990s, another was found. Neither of these skeletons - which had both been buried over a century before, were ever identified and an explanation of why they were buried under the theatre was never found.

*At the end of King Street is the Llandoger Trow. This pub will be the next location on this tour.*

## 5. The Ghosts of the Llandoger

What would an old pub be without a ghost? They're as familiar to British taverns as a roaring fire or pork scratchings and while many sightings of these apparitions can be put down to the consumption of spirits of another kind, the Llandoger Trow can boast not one, but an astonishing twelve ghosts.

The actual number of ghosts is a matter of debate among those who like to debate such things, but the Llandoger certainly has more than its fair share of stories concerning the supernatural.

The Old Vic Theatre is only a few doors up King Street from the Llandoger and because of this, the pub has had a strange mixture of regulars over the years. Actors and theatre professionals would drink alongside merchants and sailors - with the occasional pirate thrown in for good measure from time to time.

It must have been quite an extraordinary place to spend an evening, back in the 18th century, when Bristol was at its height as a trading port, so much so that for some of the pubs regulars not even death would be their final orders.

The Llandoger can boast a pair of theatrical ghosts. Sarah Siddons, the Georgian actress and tragedienne - known both for her heart-wrenching performance of Desdemona and also for playing every tragic female from Shakespeare's work - is said to make the occasional appearance. Sarah has quite a busy haunting schedule, including a handful of other pubs and at least a dozen theatres (including the Bristol Old Vic).

Another actor, Henry Irving is believed to show up from time to time. Irving was one of the most popular performers of the Victorian age and was one of the inspirations for Bram Stoker in creating the character of Count Dracula.

Another celebrity ghost is Blackbeard the pirate - the most famous (non-fiction) pirate in history, who is known to have visited the pub as a young man.

Other ghosts include old-favourites such as a monk (who is said to haunt the cellars) and a woman in white/grey, but the best known and most frequently reported ghost of them all is also the saddest.

A small boy is said to wander the upper floors of the Llandoger. What's unusual about him among the ghost world is that he's almost exclusively seen during daylight hours, often being spotted from the street, gazing down from the top floor windows. Not much is known of who this boy could've been or how he came to haunt the pub but a spiritual medium claimed a few decades back that his name was Pierre, and that name has become how he is referred to ever since.

If he exists at all, Pierre seems to be living quite a miserable afterlife. Often seen (or heard) is his creaky leg iron and he has a habit of approaching adults, as if asking for help. Perhaps most tragic of all is that poor Pierre might not even know he's even dead.

Whatever the truth of the Llandoger's ghosts, it's a beautiful, ancient pub and one of our finest. Don't let the ghosts of the past frighten you off having a pint in the present!

*We're staying at the Llandoger Trow for now, so why not head inside and treat yourself to a drink?*

## 6. The Llandoger and Selkirk

There may be debates as to whether the Llandoger Trow or the Hatchet are officially the oldest pub in Bristol, but one thing the Llandoger cannot be rivalled on is its extraordinary literary pedigree.

In Robert Louis Stevenson's 1882 masterpiece *"Treasure Island"*, the Llandoger Trow is the inspiration for the Admiral Benbow. It's quite an extraordinary experience to sit in the pub and read the passages concerning the Admiral Benbow as the place has changed so little since then that there's an uncanny feeling of actually being inside the book itself!

It is also believed to be where, sometime around 1712, Daniel Defoe met Alexander Selkirk who had been castaway on an island for many years. This encounter would encourage Defoe to write *"The Life and Surprising Adventures of Robinson Crusoe"*.

Alexander Selkirk had been a naval officer and a privateer. In 1704, he was part of a crew of men aboard the *Cinque Ports* operating in the South Pacific Ocean. Though their duties were to protect British interests overseas, the crew was not averse to the occasional bout of pillaging, should French or Spanish vessels wander too close.

After a dramatic battle with a French ship off the coast of Chile, the *Cinque Ports* landed on the uninhabited Mas a Tierra island for much needed repairs.

Selkirk, who was often petulant and impulsive, told Captain Thomas Stradling that he'd rather take his chances on the island than board the stricken vessel.

Stradling took him at his word and despite Selkirk's pleas, he was stranded on the island with nothing but a couple of knives, a change of clothes, a bedsheet and a

Bible. In October, 1704, Alexander Selkirk found himself completely alone.

Selkirk spent the first few weeks in a pit of despair, cursing his insolence and living off nothing but fruit, but once he found a herd of goats living on the island, he taught himself how to hunt and later how to build a shelter and even fashion clothing out of materials he found on the island.

He even managed to befriend some of the feral cats which roamed about the island - most likely left there by previous naval voyages. Within a year, he was fully established on the island and a self-taught expert in survival.

He would be on the island for a total of four years and four months before rescue came in the form of a British merchant ship which had landed by chance on Mas a Tierra.

Upon returning to Britain, Selkirk became a media sensation, with newspapers publishing his account in daily installments. Once the public fascination with his story began to dwindle, Selkirk settled in Bristol.

While in Bristol his impulsive nature got the better of him once more, and he was frequently imprisoned for drunken behaviour and for getting into fights with strangers. By the time Defoe met Selkirk in the Llandoger, it's believed he would tell anyone his story in exchange for a pint.

Over several nights, Defoe listened to these accounts and in 1719, *"Robinson Crusoe"* was first published.

Defoe's classic novel, inspired by Selkirk's astonishing story would probably never have existed had it not been for a chance encounter between the two men in the Llandoger Trow, whereupon one of Bristol's oldest and best-loved pubs earned its place in literary history.

On Queen Charlotte Street, you should be able to see the Granary Building, a red building with a highly decorative exterior. This will be our next location on the tour.

## 7. Bristol Byzantine

The Granary, the dazzlingly confident red brick building between Welshback and Queen Charlotte Street is regarded as the jewel in the crown as far as the short-lived but hugely popular Bristol Byzantine architectural style is concerned.

It was built in 1869, at the height of the city's fondness for this movement. The first example of the style is believed to have been the Arnolfini, and its appealing form seems to have sparked something of a revolution in design across the city.

From 1850 until the 1880s, Bristol Byzantine was the primary architectural style of newly constructed buildings in Bristol. The style, which blended Moorish and Byzantine iconography with Gloucestershire stone worked especially well for the design of warehouses, as its uniform symmetry and reliance on circular forms could create remarkably robust buildings on a huge scale which were also aesthetically pleasing.

The Granary was designed by Archibald Pontin and William Venn Gough, who together and separately, created some other fine examples of the style which can be found nearby on Bathurst Basin and along the feeder canal.

The reason for the style's popularity was clear. Not only was it an attractive and distinct design, but with the decline of the city as a port of international importance, Bristol felt as if it had lost its identity somewhat - and here was an architectural style that the city could lay claim to.

It was a style the city fully embraced and at one point there seems to barely have been any buildings at all that weren't constructed with this aesthetic - so much so that its popularity began to fade. Perhaps people simply desired variety again.

Many of the finest Bristol Byzantine buildings were lost during the early years of the 20th century, as the city expanded and The Blitz claimed many more, but the masterpiece of the Granary was saved and continues to be regarded as the most magnificent example of its style and also one of the finest buildings in the city.

There is a persistent rumour that the basement of the Granary, where a pub is located, was where in 1989, the episode of *"Only Fools of Horses"* where Del Boy falls through the bar was filmed. Sadly, this rumour is only half true.

In the episode, entitled *"Yuppy Love"* the exterior of the building was used but the wine bar where the classic moment in British TV history happened, was actually filmed in a studio.

*We're off to Queen Square next. Follow the road on the north side of the Square about three quarters of the way along. There is a building called Custom House here and it is the subject of our next stop.*

## 8. The Queen Square Riot

Queen Square was built in 1699 as living quarters for the wealthy elite and has been consistently thought of as one of the most handsome city squares in the country ever since.

Though it may seem a tranquil haven from the bustle of urban living, this charming green space was the scene of one of the bloodiest and brutal riots in our city's history.

Before the riot in 1831, tensions between the haves and have-nots had been mounting for some time and the balance of power seemed to be entirely out of the hands of the working people of the city. Out of a population of 104,000 people, only 6,000 of them were even permitted to vote - all of whom were wealthy, and of course, none of whom were women.

As the rich got richer and the poor were exploited and without a voice, it was clear that something radical was going to happen, and it happened on the 29th of October of 1831, when Sir Charles Wetherall visited friends in the city.

Wetherall was a local magistrate, who had been a staunch opponent of a parliamentary bill which would have given more people the vote - and had helped stall the bill's progress into law.

Immediately upon his arrival in the city, he was met by a gang of young men, who jeered him and according to some accounts, threw rocks. The terrified man fled for his life to where the current Custom House now stands, while a mob began to form outside the building.

Wetherall managed to escape in disguise (depending who you believe, this was either dressed as a woman or a pauper) but the mob refused to believe he had gone, even when the people trapped inside Custom House taped boards to the windows which read *"CHARLES WETHERALL HAS LEFT BRISTOL"*.

When the crowd was finally addressed from the top story of the building, they erupted with fury. All around the square, windows were smashed and then fires were lit.

By nightfall, much of the north end of the park was ablaze and over 500 men were now attempting to force entry into Custom House. The riots went beyond Queen Square and to Bristol New Gaol on Cumberland Road, which was soon surrounded. The prison was partially destroyed and dozens of inmates released, while a gang of men hurled the city's gallows into the nearby New Cut.

The riots continued for three days and nights, despite a massive police presence - some of whom had been sworn in as special officers solely to help quell the insurgence.

It only ended sometime after Custom House, which had by then been seized and set alight, finally collapsed. Many of the bodies which would be found inside would never be identified.

The official tally counted the number of injured at 86 and the dead at four - though both of those figures are believed to be considerably lower than the actual number.

Five of the supposed ringleaders were hanged in what was now the ruins of the New Gaol and the entire city was put on curfew for several nights.

It took a long time for the laws to change and for more of the city's population to be enfranchised by the vote, but the Queen Square riot of 1831 set in motion a rebalance of power which would come to embolden much of the people of Bristol.

Perhaps most importantly, it taught those in positions of authority over the city that they should always be a little frightened of the power of people.

*We're now heading towards the magnificent statue in the centre of Queen Square.*

## 9. The Secret of the King William III Statue

The centrepiece of Queen Square has been described many times as one of the finest equestrian statues to be found in Europe.

Michael Rysbrack's 1736 depiction of King William III is a breathtaking masterpiece. Cast in bronze and on an enormous plinth, it has been one of the most celebrated statues in Bristol for almost three hundred years.

It's astonishing to think that from the 1930s until 1999, the statue overlooked a completely different Queen Square - one which had a duel carriageway diagonally across it, with the King William statue on an island in the middle of the road. This act of cultural vandalism is often seen as one of the greatest crimes against Bristol ever committed by the council and a completely insensitive means to go about solving traffic issues.

Mercifully Queen Square was returned to its original design just in time for the millennium and the park you see today looks pretty much identical to how it would have been when it was built in 1699 (with a few houses, especially on the north side, replacements for ones destroyed in the 1831 riot).

Michael Rysbrack's statue was deemed so important to the morale of the city, that in the buildup to WWII, it was moved to a secret location for several years in case of an attack from German aircraft. When the attacks did come, the Square was largely spared and the statue was returned with a huge fanfare in 1945 - an event which many saw at the time as the city's own VE Day.

As popular a monument as it is, few people seem to be aware that it hides a rather strange detail. It may actually be a depiction of the moment a king is about to die. William III suffered a less than noble death when, in 1702, his horse stumbled over a molehill. His injuries would later kill him.

If you look closely under the right, back hoof of the horse, you will see a mound which some people have suggested may represent the molehill which changed the course of history.

In London's St James' Park there is a near identical statue to Michael Rysbrack's version, in which the molehill is made to appear more evident, and a nearby Jacobean society, formed in the years before William III's death still begin every meeting with a toast to the statue - or more particularly, a toast to who they call "the little man in the velvet waistcoat" - the humble mole who took down a king.

*In the southwest corner of Queen Square you will find the Hole in the Wall, a pub and restaurant. Towards the rear there is a small anteroom jutting out of the exterior, in which there is a pair of narrow windows.*

## 10. The Hole in the Wall

The pub on the edge of Queen Square and Welshback is the Hole in Wall - a charming, historic establishment which hides a rather unusual secret.

It is thought to be the inspiration for the Spyglass Inn in Robert Louis Stevenson's classic *Treasure Island,* which features in the chapter where Jim Hawkins and Long John Silver have their fateful first encounter. The restaurant within the pub is named the Spyglass in honour of its literary heritage.

Due to its location, on the bend of the Floating Harbour, it was popular with sailors during the 18th century and likely drew a slightly wealthier crowd, as the stretch of water which runs along the Grove side of the road has been known as the Mud Dock for centuries and had the most expensive moorings in the city.

When the tidal Avon ran through Bristol, the riverbed below consisted mostly of jagged rocks. Mooring your vessel at high tide was always risky, as when the tide ebbed, a ship could find herself perilously placed on a stony crag which had been hidden from sight. However, the Mud Dock was a strip of the waterway which had a naturally occurring silt bank laying over any rocky outcrops. At low tide, ships would be softly cushioned along this bank and you could be confident that your vessel would survive the tidal change.

It is along the Grove side of the Hole in the Wall where you can find the pub's most unusual feature. The small room affixed to the back of the building is currently used as a very welcoming snug, but in the 18th century when it was built, it served a vital role in ensuring the safety of the pub's clientele.

It is a spy-hole, used to watch over the city for the approach of the hated press gangs - groups of men who were assigned to "coerce" unemployed sailors onto ships. While legally, they were meant only to use powers of persuasion, in reality these gangs were often violent and forceful, often dragging men onto vessels against their will to ensure that a ship had a seaworthy crew.

International trade was not always a return journey, and oftentimes ships would jettison much of their crew to allow room for extra supplies they had picked up along the way. Sailors would regularly be abandoned in ports whilst other times, ships would find themselves bereft of crew before beginning voyages.

Perhaps the sneakiest tactic used by the press gangs was also their most successful. They would approach pubs that were known to be frequented by sailors and regardless of whether or not they were already in the employ of another captain, would ply the sailors with drink until they fell unconscious. The press gangs would haul their bodies onboard ships and the hapless sailor would awake the following morning and discover, to his horror that he was now aboard a ship which was headed for the other side of the world.

The spy-hole was intended to give the drinkers of the Hole in the Wall a warning of their approach, so that they could either flee, or try their luck against the wits of the press gangs.

*That concludes our tour of King Street and Queen Square. The following walk is themed around statues and tells the lesser-known stories of some of the people Bristol has sought to memorialise in sculpture over the years. It begins in Millennium Square, which can be found by walking to the southwest corner of Queen Square and crossing the harbour using Pero's Bridge (the footbridge with huge horns at either side). Heading in a straight line after the bridge will take you to Millennium Square. Look for a statue here of movie star Cary Grant.*

# Walk Nine
## Statues

# Statues

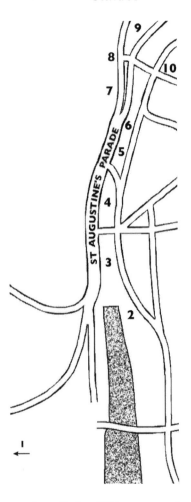

This chapter is a little different to the others, as it is solely concerned with the statues which can be found in a trail leading from Millennium Square to the edge of Broadmead.

Statues, when they are displayed in public, are historically important as they give us an indication of who the city saw fit to celebrate at various points in time. Of them, we will be visiting a Hollywood legend with a heartbreakingly sad story of his early life in Bristol, a Roman god who suddenly gained a potbelly in the Victorian era and of course, the most controversial statue in all of Bristol, the presence of which, continues to divide the city.

# 1. The Sad Story of Archibald Leach

In the years preceding the millennium, a committee was formed in the city to discuss who from the history of Bristol should be commemorated in statue as part of the new Millennium Square. The committee concluded that boy-poet Thomas Chatterton, William Tyndale - whose translation of the Bible into English was seen as blasphemous enough for him to be executed, William Penn - the governor who Pennsylvania is named after and Hollywood megastar Cary Grant.

Grant may seem a little incongruous in this company, seeing as he is the only one to have lived in recent memory, but there is no doubt that he has earned a place among the luminaries of Bristol's history.

Cary Grant (1904-1986) was born Archibald Leach in Horfield to parents Elias and Elsie Leach. From an early age, Archie showed an interest in performance and his mother enrolled him in acting classes at the age of six. It's generally believed that his love of acting may have stemmed from needing means to escape the distresses of his home life.

Archibald's father was a violent alcoholic, often spending long stretches of time away from home, while his mother suffered from mental health problems which would likely be diagnosed as a bi-polar disorder today.

Following one of his father's extended absences, Archibald Leach was surprised one afternoon when, having come home Bishop Road Primary School, his father was waiting for him. Archie was informed that his mother had gone on a long holiday and would not be coming home soon - then a few weeks later he was told that his mother had died on this trip of a mysterious illness.

Poor Archie was devastated. His father had little ability or interest in raising the child, so he was put into the care of his grandparents who lived on Picton Street, Montpelier. It was at this time that Archie joined a theatre troupe and began performing at venues across the city.

At the age of fourteen, he was expelled from his grammar school - the explanation for this was later given that he'd been caught spying on the girls changing rooms but this is likely a Hollywood invention. At this point he was able to dedicate himself full-time to becoming a performer (most biographers agree that whatever led to Archie's expulsion, it was probably intentional for this very reason.)

Soon Archie was part of a vaudeville group who performed on cruise ships. It was here that movie legends Mary Pickford and Douglas Fairbanks spotted the young man's potential and invited him to Los Angeles. The rest, of course, is history.

But Archibald's relationship with Bristol was not over. In the 1930's, now an accomplished and famous actor with the Hollywood-approved name of Cary Grant, he returned to Britain to visit his ailing father who, on his deathbed, offered a shocking confession.

Archie's mother hadn't died. She had been sent to Glenside Mental Hospital (now UWE's Glenside Campus). Stigma surrounding mental health was so extreme, that Elias Leach believed his son would rather hear his mother had died than had been institutionalised.

After several years, Archibald negotiated his mother's release from the hospital, and for the rest of her life, the man who would become one of the greatest leading men in film history financially supported her and returned to his childhood home whenever he could.

Bristol had further tragedies to inflict upon Archibald Leach. During the blitz he lost his aunt, uncle, cousin and her husband, as well as their infant son.

For understandable reasons, Archibald Leach did not harbour warm memories of Bristol, but Bristol certainly remembers him - as one of our finest ever sons.

*Return over Pero's Bridge and take a left turn. This stretch of the harbour leading towards St Augustine's Parade is called Broad Quay. At the end of it, you will find a circular fountain, featuring the figures of two men on one side and a lion's head on the other.*

## 2. The "Frankenstein" Fountain

Although it is officially registered as a memorial to King George V, the fountain between Broad Quay and St Augustine's Parade can be fairly described as signifying absolutely nothing…

On one side there is a lion's head, which occasionally squirts water into a circular basin, while on the other are two men, one seemingly a farmer who's harvesting corn and the other a miner with a pickaxe. It may be hard to imagine how this imagery was intended to glorify the long-dead king when it was unveiled in 1982, but that's because there was no intention to.

About fifty years previously, there had been calls for public donations to support the construction of a memorial to the king, but the final tally was a slender amount. Poor George V is the kind of monarch usually spoken of with words such as "adequate" and "mediocre" and has never attracted the kind of devotion our more sensational royals have.

Nevertheless, the interest on the donation gathered over the intervening years and by the early 1980s it was a somewhat substantial amount. Plans were put in place for some kind of dedication to the king but even with interest, the money would not stretch far.

The solution was that rather than build a memorial from scratch, one could be cheaply cobbled together using masonry which had been stored after the demolition of the nearby Co-operative Society Headquarters, which stood where Broad Quay House can now be found.

In 1981, the salvaged sculptures were assembled together in a kind of early form of upcycling and the resulting fountain was presented to a disinterested city the following year.

Despite being described as a "Frankenstein's Monster" of a sculpture in a letter to a local newspaper, the fountain is a quite a charming oddity on the waterfront, which provides a delightful place to sit beneath leafy trees on a sunny day - just don't try interpreting what any of its symbolism is supposed to mean!

*Our next statue is in sight of this fountain. Neptune cannot be missed, staring out at the harbour from a plinth on St Augustine's Parade.*

## 3. Neptune

One of the best loved and easily recognised statues in the city, is also among its very oldest.

Sculpted in 1721 by artist John Randall (also known as Joseph), the statue of Neptune now standing dramatically over St Augustine's Parade is cast entirely in lead and stands upon a gigantic wedge of granite, quarried from Dartmoor.

Neptune has experienced quite a few changes of scenery over his lifetime, not least of all the radical changes which have happened to the city over the past three hundred years, but he has been placed in six different locations around Bristol - more than any of our other statues.

He wasn't placed on St Augustine's Parade until 1999. Before that, he had overlooked Temple Church, Bristol Bridge and what's now Broadmead. At one point he was even used as the unofficial mascot of a nautical market stall, which was set up beneath him and sold goods for sailors before they set out for voyages on the high seas. Most people seem to agree that Neptune - the god of the sea, who has long been associated with Bristol's seafarers - seems best suited to be gazing out to the harbour.

Closer inspection of this handsome sculpture may reveal why lead is such an infrequently used material for outdoor statues. Lead has a habit of softening when exposed to rain, so a lot of Neptune's features have faded over time.

Worse still are the effects on the inside. Rain had been leaching away the core of the statue for over a century by the start of the Victorian era, and Neptune was starting to look somewhat limp, as he was almost hollow and sagging under his own weight.

The solution was an easy, if somewhat crude one. Neptune's head was lopped off and into his neck was poured liquid concrete. This solved the issue of his hollow innards, the new problem was that whoever was responsible for this repair, hadn't taken into account how much concrete was necessary, so Neptune has been left with somewhat of a pot belly!

*With the harbour and ferry landing behind you, walk forwards until you find the statue of man with his right arm in the air. There is a dedication to "Burke" inscribed on his plinth.*

## 4. Edward Burke

Often described as appearing to be either waving at a friend or hailing a taxi, the 1894 bronze statue of politician Edmund Burke (1729-1797), by acclaimed sculptor James Harvard Thomas is often overlooked somewhat - being placed between more celebrated/provocative works, but it's a grand piece of sculpture for a distinguished man who deserves celebration.

Burke served as an MP for Bristol for a relatively short space of time (1774-1780) but is regarded as a very influential figure in British politics for his oratory skills and unflappable sense of justice.

As a child, Burke first came to Bristol from his birthplace of Dublin due to a catalogue of ailments that were inflicting the small boy. The warm, natural spas found in Hotwells were believed by some to have curative powers and young Edward was often required to spend several hours a day soaking in the waters (waters we now know to be highly toxic.)

It is claimed that the boy made a remarkable recovery from his maladies and his family spent the following years living between Dublin, Bristol and London.

During his election campaign in 1774, Burke proved to be a divisive figure, not least of all because he claimed to be largely blasé about representing the interests of Bristol alone in parliament and wanted to contribute to improving the nation as a whole. Burke also split the electorate by openly speaking out against the slave trade, hoping to implement restrictions which would eventually lead to its complete abolition.

His electoral win was all the more remarkable considering only a small percentage of the city were actually eligible to vote, and many of those who could were personally invested in the city's links to the slave trade.

However, he was said to be an incredibly persuasive speaker, which must have contributed greatly to his success.

One famous speech he gave to Bristol included the lines which are now inscribed into the plinth upon which his statue stands. "I wish to be a member of Parliament to have my share of doing good and resisting evil."

Burke is known to have had a preoccupation with the concepts of good and evil, believing that they were not necessarily the result of good or bad people, but their actions.

It is likely for this reason that Burke is often incorrectly attributed to the quote "The only thing necessary for the triumph of evil is for good men to do nothing" - but this was actually coined by British philosopher John Stuart Mill, 70 years after Burke's death.

Burke went on to represent Melton in Yorkshire as a Member of Parliament and later served as Paymaster of the Forces under George III and then Rector of the University of Glasgow.

Still remembered as one of the greatest public speakers in history, his statue in Bristol has fallen into disrepair somewhat. Suffering shrapnel damage during WWII and a gunshot wound in 1980s. However, this damage has led to something quite extraordinary, as if you look closely on summer days, you may well see bees buzzing around the man's right armpit.

He has (at this time of writing) become an enormous, human-shaped bronze beehive, with a colony of potentially thousands of honey bees living inside of him…

*Here goes. We're heading to the most controversial statue in Bristol. Continue moving away from the harbour and the next statue you should see is of Edward Colston…*

## 5. The Colston Statue

*There are few things as daunting to write about in Bristol's history as Edward Colston, the massively divisive figure whose statue, which stares benignly - even plaintively over Augustine's Parade, is easily our most controversial historical figure.*

*For this installment I want to stick to the known facts of the man, but before I do so, I think it's important to declare my own bias on the matter - as it's near impossible for a writer not to let his or her own opinions creep onto the page.*

*I believe there is a place for the statue of Edward Colston in Bristol, but that place is in a museum, where the man can be contextualised properly against his deeds (good and bad).*

*With that out of the way, I shall try to proceed with the lid on this can of worms firmly in place.*

Edward Colston was born in Bristol on the 2nd of November, 1636. His father was High Sheriff of Bristol and his family had long ties to the city. The youngest of fifteen children, the family left Bristol around about the time of the English Civil War, where they spent the war years in the countryside before moving to London soon after it had concluded.

In his early twenties, Edward began working for a trades and exports company, selling wine and cloth to European countries. By 1680, he had come to the attention of the Royal African Company and began working for them soon afterwards.

The Royal African Company had initially been founded as a mining company to take advantage of a seam of gold which had been found in west Africa but soon afterwards, they discovered that there was more money to be made - and a more dependable source of "goods" to be found in the trade of human beings.

In 1689, Colston was now the director of the Royal African Company and it was at this time that he decided to break London's monopoly on the slave trade and to fund expeditions along the Triangular Trade Route from Bristol. This route took British goods and money overseas to African countries and exchanged them for captured slaves, who were then shipped off to the Americas where they were exchanged for the bounties of plantations such as sugar and tobacco which were then brought back to Britain.

It was an endless, massively profitable international exchange from which Colston made an enormous personal fortune, but the statistics behind it are harrowing.

The Royal African Company alone was responsible for the forced transportation of over 84,000 slaves, of whom 12,000 were children. Of these slaves about 19,000 died in the squalid conditions on transit to America. On top of this, Edward Colston is believed to have personally funded countless voyages with his own money and using his own ships - we don't know how many slaves were transported in these voyages.

Colston never returned to Bristol but donated a great deal of money to the city in his later life. These donations went to founding hospitals, almshouses and schools across the city and whilst this generosity cannot be denied, it was often not an unconditional act of philanthropy.

In 1702, he offered a donation of money which would be a sum of multi-millions in contemporary pounds to one of the city's largest schools, but with a proviso that the school end its current practice of allowing children of all different religious affiliations to attend and instead allow only the children of Church of England families admittance. The school politely declined his offer.

In 1710, Edward Colston became an MP for Bristol, a position he held for only one parliamentary term. During this time, Colston found himself, for the first time, having to defend his business interests against a burgeoning abolition movement. At the time, most of the people of Britain weren't aware of the extent of the slave trade but over the following years and decades, opposition would grow - particularly in Bristol - despite the city having profited so much from it.

Soon after his stint in Parliament, Colston retired. He died in his home in 1721.

For many years, the legacy of Colston seemed to have died with him, and though he was fondly remembered by the city, his character was reappraised by Victorian Bristol society, who began to depict him less as an investor and more of a heroic explorer (despite there being scant evidence that he took part in any voyages at all). Fanciful legends of the man's life were soon being reported as fact, such as a tale where Colston and his crew were rescued by friendly dolphins when their ship overturned at sea - which is why dolphins are featured around the base of his statue.

The statue itself was erected in 1895 and was designed by renowned sculptor John Cassidy. There does not seem to have been much opposition to this statue at the time but with the end of the Victorian era, Colston once again began to slide into historical irrelevance once more.

It has only been in recent decades that Edward Colston's role not just in the slave trade, but as as Bristolian hero has been reappraised.

While it's often argued that we are judging a man using our contemporary sensibilities, he was still a man who oversaw an unbelievable amount of death and suffering. It's only reasonable that we should ask, with those very same contemporary sensibilities, if it's reasonable to have a statue seeming to celebrate the man's legacy - or if so many buildings, streets and institutions should be named in his honour.

*Onto lighter subjects next. Continue on from the Colston statue and to the left of the war memorial you should see a stone, cuboid structure with an open top. It is a horse trough, and the story of why it is here is a very sweet, but almost forgotten one.*

## 6. The Horse Trough

Rarely noticed at the northern end of The Centre, in an area known as Magpie Park beside St Augustine's Parade is a nine-foot long granite trough.

It was installed here in 1910 at the request of Captain Richard B. Nicholetts as his final act of charity.

Nicholetts had, for many years, been the master of a rather unusual school near Portishead. Moored just off of the coast, the HMS Formidable served as a kind of floating boarding school in the Bristol Channel, where neglected and underprivileged boys were educated in all subjects, but with a particular emphasis on naval training.

The battleship HMS Formidable was built in 1825 but it's likely that it never served in conflict. In 1869 it was repurposed into the National Nautical School - a school entirely funded by charitable donations which attempted to offer boys who would otherwise be denied one an education.

The school was notorious, even for its age, for the strictness and discipline with which the boys were treated and there are accounts of boys jumping overboard in an attempt to flee the floating school - two of whom are believed to have drowned in their attempts.

However, the master of the school from 1890-1901, Captain Nicholetts, was regarded as a friendly, amiable chap who most of the boys were very fond of. The captain was famed for his love of animals and he is said to have kept a small menagerie of creatures both onboard and at his home.

After retiring from teaching, Captain Nicholetts spent his final years campaigning against the practice of animal vivisection in schools, which he found both pointless and cruel and it is thought that both he and his wife became vegetarians after his retirement - a practice almost unheard of at the time.

He died in 1908 and his wife continued his campaigns against cruelty to animals for the rest of her life. In his will he offered a moderate sum of money in the hope of leaving a legacy for Bristol which would help animals, and thus the horse trough was made.

Although it's been badly weathered by the elements, you can just about make out an inscription in dedication to the captain which reads *"In grateful memory of Captain R. B. Nicholetts R. N. who died August 24th 1908. This trough is erected for the use of animals, of whom he was always the unfailing friend and champion. Blessed are the merciful."*

It is a lovely memorial to a man who, even in death, wanted to offer his kindness to animals.

*Keep following St Augustine's Parade towards Christmas Steps. Near to the bottom of the steps there is an archway, sealed off with a metal gate. Through here you should be able to make out a blackened and eroded statue, about a foot tall affixed to the wall.*

## 7. The Beheaded Virgin

At the bottom of Christmas Steps and through the railings which seal off St Bartholomew's Gateway, there is a rather curious statue on the wall.

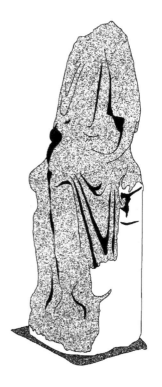

Worn and weathered with time, it may be hard to work out what this figure represents, but she is the Virgin Mary - and she is without a head.

It's believed that she is cradling baby Jesus, but it is very difficult to discern where this baby could be. It's been suggested that this may once have been part of a larger nativity scene but no evidence of that has ever been found.

However, if it were true, it would not be the only nativity imagery to be found in the area. At the top of Christmas Steps is the Chapel of the Three Kings - which also serves as the church for the almshouses which can be found there.

The chapel is named in honour of the Three Kings of Cologne and likenesses of the trio, bearing gifts for the Christ Child, can be found on the exterior wall which meets the almshouses. This church and these depictions of the wise men may have given Christmas Steps its unusual name.

The more commonly suggested reason for Christmas Steps name is that it comes from a corruption of "Knifesmith" as the area was for a long time renowned for metalworking, particularly in making knives, and knifesmithing was a common term for this practice.

The statue of the Virgin Mary is believed to date back to somewhere around 1240, making it by some margin, the oldest surviving statue in Bristol.

If you look closely, you will see that the feet of the Virgin Mary have turned completely black and it's believed that this is due to centuries of pious worshipers having touched the stone for a blessing.

The obvious question about the statue is, of course, why does she have no head? That part is a bit of a mystery but there is a very popular and often repeated explanation that just might happen to be true.

The rumour is that the statue was beheaded by none other than Oliver Cromwell. He is said to have gone into a fit of rage at what he perceived as Catholic idolatry and lopped the Virgin's head off with a single swipe of his sword. It's also been suggested that this vandalism was an act of revenge, due to Bristol's neutral stance during the English Civil War.

Could it be true? Maybe. Cromwell certainly came to Bristol and spent some time here. It was a strategically important city during the Civil War and the man is believed to have had something of a habit of desecrating religious iconography. In the absence of evidence pointing to another explanation, I suggest the Cromwell theory is as good as any other!

*Very close to St Bartholomew's Gate there is a statue of a rather sickly looking man on a horse. He will be our next stop.*

## 8. The Cloaked Horseman

Beside Lewin's Mead is a strikingly sombre statue. Sculpted in 1984 by acclaimed artist David Blackhouse, it is named "Cloaked Horseman" and it marks an important chapter in Bristol's history.

Compared to the most famous equestrian statue in the city, King William III in Queen Square, there is a stark contrast - for even the horse here appears tired and forlorn. If you follow the mans wearied gaze, you will see that he is aligned to appear as if he is staring through the gateway of the old wall. We are meant to take this as a suggestion that he is a traveller, arriving at the outskirts of a fortified city.

Had he actually been standing here at that time, his horse would be neck deep in water, as the River Frome flowed across this very spot until the city was built over the top of it. The river continues underground for quite some distance.

Close to where the statue can be found once stood St Bartholomew's Hospital. Built in 1220, it was one of the country's first ever free hospitals and offered treatments for conditions as mild as headaches to as serious as leprosy.

It's unlikely that any of these treatments actually helped patients. These were the days when medical interventions meant leeches, bloodletting and elixirs which were little more than coloured water, but the hospital remained on this spot for at least three hundred years and treated thousands of patients, many of whom were travellers from afar who had journeyed to the city in hope of a miracle cure.

The Cloaked Horseman is intended to represent such a traveller and he remains a poignant reminder of the sick and dying, but it was also intended to be a celebra-

237

tion of our nation's history of free healthcare. By marking the origins of Britain's fledgling medical history, it was also meant to remind us all of the precious good fortune we have of living in a country where healthcare remains free, at the point of use, for all people, from the cradle to the grave.

*The next statue on this tour can be found close by. Still following the street, you should see a small, triangular park which sits as an island between roads. Over it, you will see the figure of a man on a pedestal. This unsung hero will be our next stop.*

## 9. Samuel Morley

Whenever the controversy over the Colston statue flares up again, one of the frequently asked questions from the general public is, if the statue was moved, what would replace it?

I have no doubt that the Edward Colston statue will eventually become a museum piece, at which time, I hope the Samuel Morley sculpture beside Lewin's Mead is considered for its replacement, because this seldom-seen memorial on a rather neglected scrap of grass really should be displayed more prominently, as he was one of the city's finest.

Morley was born into a wealthy Nottingham family in 1809. The family had found riches through the manufacturing and selling of underwear. In 1860, Samuel inherited the company from his deceased father and he went about turning the company into an international distributor.

Morley became tremendously wealthy, but he was also a philanthropist who believed it was the duty of the rich to help those who could not help themselves. Annually, he donated between £20,000 and £30,000 - which is the modern day equivalent to £1.5 to £2.3 million to charities, many of which were based in Bristol. Not least of these was a huge donation to Bristol Cathedral in order that much needed repairs and maintenance could continue.

Throughout his life, Samuel Morley was associated with quite radically progressive politics, especially in matters regarding the poor, who he believed were in that position for faults of the nation rather than any personal failings. In 1868 he represented Bristol as an MP, which was a position he held until his retirement in 1885.

He is recalled as being quite an austere and formal man, who laughed infrequently and made friends rarely. He did however, keep correspondences with people all over the world, and it is perhaps his friendship with Josiah Henson with which he will most be remembered.

Born onto a plantation in Maryland in 1789, Josiah Henson had been a slave who first came to the attention of Samuel Morley when he penned a letter to British abolitionists in 1830, explaining his story. Henson had escaped the plantation in the dead of night and was currently a wanted criminal in America for having done so. He had successfully crossed the border into Canada, via the Niagara River and was now seeking donations to start a school which could educate other slaves who had escaped their lives of entrapment.

Morley's family had been anti-slavery campaigners for some time and the letter found its way to Samuel a few years after it had been written. Samuel became something of a benefactor to Josiah and eventually the treasurer of a charity which had been set up to help fund the school.

The school, which also housed a settlement for fugitives, was eventually home to over 500 people who had escaped slavery in America.

Morley stayed in touch with Henson until Henson's death in 1883, aged 93. Morley continued supporting what became known as the Dawn Settlement, along with similar establishments in Canada, until he himself died in 1886, at the age of 77.

Having served as an MP for almost 20 years and as a philanthropist who donated huge sums of money to the city, Samuel Morley deserves greater recognition - but it is as an abolitionist for which he should be remembered as a Bristol hero.

*Return to the cloaked horseman statue and follow his gaze to the gateway. On the opposite side (Broad Street) there are two figures above the arch.*

## 10. Brennus and Bellinus

Above the archway on the eastern side of the magnificent gateway which leads to Broad Street are the figures of two men, each wearing a crown and holding a sceptre. These are the mythical brothers Brennus and Bellinus who, according to legend, first founded the city of Bristol.

They are considerably newer additions to the gateway, which is actually part of the tower belonging to St John on-the-wall church, which was built sometime in the 13th century and are believed to have been sculpted sometime around the year 1700.

This section of the old wall is all that survives of a fortification which one encircled the entirety of Old Town, to see the city and its inhabitants safe from attack - and outsiders. It was also the gateway through which Queen Elizabeth I, in 1574 and Queen Victoria, in 1899 entered Old Town.

Brennus and Bellinus are two characters who once played a major part in myths and legends of old England, much like King Arthur, but unlike the King of Camelot, these brothers have almost been forgotten.

The legend goes that they were the twin sons of the first king of England. They travelled around the country for many years getting into all kinds of unlikely but heroic adventures, all the while building an army of Britons which they then led across Europe towards Italy in 391 BC.

Once there, they set about destroying the Roman Empire and almost burnt Rome itself to the ground. They returned to England victorious and soon afterwards founded a settlement upon a hill, which they named "Bristut". It would later become known as Brigstowe and then later still, Bristol.

242

Unlike the myth of the giant brothers, Vincent and Goram, whose rivalry in love lead to the creation of the Avon Gorge, this was a legend which was not only claimed to be true, but belief in it appears to have been widespread.

In the late 15th century book *The Maire of Brigstowe is Kalendar* ("The Mayor's Calendar") the author, Bristol town clerk Robert Ricart repeats the story as the true manner in which the city was founded. The book itself is a fascinating relic of a bygone age, documenting life in Bristol during the late 1400s, and features one of the first ink-and-paper (as opposed to etched on stone) city maps to be found anywhere in the world.

Of course, we now know that Bristol was founded many centuries later than the legend would have us believe, but the presence of Brennus and Bellinus is a nice reminder of the kind of myth-making about itself the city has occasionally indulged in.

*That concludes this tour. The final walk in this book takes us through part of Broadmead and into Castle Park and its neighbouring streets. That walk begins on the other side of the gateway. Close by, near to the entrance of the church built within the wall, there is a drinking fountain. This will be where the next - and final, tour begins.*

# Walk Ten
## Around Castle Park

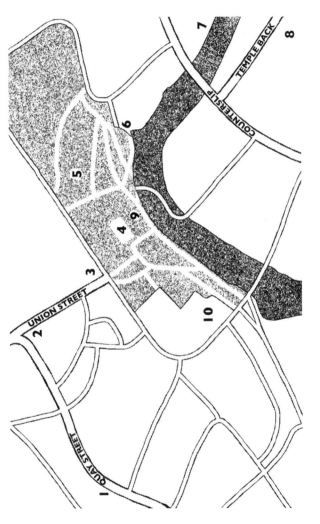

Our final tour around the city takes in an eclectic mix of sights around beautiful Castle Park. This walk has a particular focus on the Second World War, for reasons which will become evident on the walk, but also features a few lesser-known locations with stories you might not have heard before.

On this tour we will be visiting, among other things, the site of one of the city's most intriguing unsolved murders, the ruined church where a man was once exorcised of seven demons by seven holy men and the remains of a gigantic castle which once dominated the Bristol skyline.

# 1. St John's Conduit

On the Quay Street side of the old wall there is what appears to be a drinking fountain - though it's little more than a single tap jutting out of the stonework. It may not seem like much, but this was once among the most important sources of water in the city.

Although it's been a little neglected over the years, and looks in need of a bit of a spruce up, the little hollow built into the wall was the primary outlet for St John's conduit.

The conduit was an ingenious piece of medieval engineering. Dating back to 1374 - when the city was practically a child and was almost entirely ringed by a wall - it took advantage of a naturally occurring spring on Brandon Hill and, using a series of underground pipes, channels and cisterns, used gravity to draw water into the city.

The outlet was originally inside St John on-the-Wall church but was moved outside sometime during the Tudor period to allow it to be more accessible. It proved to be of vital importance to the city, as no longer would the residents have to visit the River Frome each morning to fill a bucket, and it was a reliable, relatively clean source of water which has been credited with helping the city develop into what it is today.

An even older water conduit flows to St Mary Redcliffe. The Redcliffe Conduit begins at Ashley Hill and has an outlet on the outside wall of the churchyard that can be seen close to the pavement on the Redcliff Hill side. This conduit was completed in 1207 and is probably the oldest in the city.

St John's conduit's importance may have faded with the invention of modern plumbing during the Victorian era, which allowed homes to have access to their own water supply, but it was to prove vital again during WWII.

After the blitz, which claimed most of Castle Park and much of Old Town, the bombs had not just destroyed homes, but also the plumbing infrastructure which ran below the streets. As a result, the people of the area were without water. It was at this time that the long-forgotten conduit was found to be in perfect working order and, for several weeks, became the only water source available in the city centre.

About halfway up Park Street, there is a small marker affixed into the pavement with the words "St John's Conduit" - this marker is a small reminder to those who happen to spot it, that at that very point, the hugely significant conduit still runs directly beneath their feet.

*Continue along Quay Street, moving away from the Centre. At the corner where it meets Union Street, you will find the Odeon Cinema.*

## 2. The Unsolved Murder at the Odeon.

The Odeon in Broadmead is the oldest surviving cinema in Bristol. Built as the most state-of-the-art and luxurious picture house in the city, it has been entertaining people since 1939.

When it first opened, visiting the cinema was many people's primary form of entertainment. It was affordable to virtually everybody but still had an air of glamour about it. For this reason, the average person in Britain visited the cinema about three times a week, and the Odeon was built to be the largest the city had ever seen, with almost 2,000 seats to accommodate this thirst for movie magic.

However, in 1946, the Odeon became the scene of one of the strangest unsolved murders in our history.

On the evening of the 26th of May, a packed out theatre were watching a film adaptation of Rudyard Kipling's story "The Light That Failed" - which had been made in 1939 but delayed because of the war.

1,800 people were in the cinema, 1,000 in the stalls and 800 in the slightly more expensive balcony level. The picture house manager was 33 year old father of one, Robert Parrington-Jackson and at about 6.20pm it's believed he was in his office behind the auditorium.

He was shot once in the head, possibly while seated at his desk. The gunshot is thought to have been timed to coincide with a shooting in the film, to mask the sound.

At about 6.40pm, Parrington-Jackson was discovered on the floor of his office by a cinema worker. He was alive but unconscious. The film was immediately stopped and a message asking if there was a doctor in the house was flashed up on the screen.

An ambulance arrived about five minutes later and the injured man was rushed to the Bristol Royal Infirmary but he died of his wound soon afterwards.

Rumours abounded that Robert Parrington-Jackson had been involved in some shady dealings with criminals, or that he'd secretly been having an affair with another woman, but these rumours seem to have been without substance. The theory which began to emerge is that the manager may have simply been unfortunate enough to be the victim of a robbery which went wrong.

This claim was bolstered in 1989, when a Welshman named Billy Fisher apparently confessed to the murder on his deathbed. Fisher claimed that he, along with an unnamed accomplice, had intended to rob the cinema's safe (thought to have held about £25,000 in today's money) but were interrupted by the manager, and in a panic, Fisher shot him.

Although this story was reported to the police by his son, Billy Fisher was something of a teller of tall tales, so doubt has been cast over the credibility of his claim and the case officially remains the oldest unsolved murder in Bristol history.

Screen Three of the Odeon, and the corridor which leads to it, is claimed to still be haunted by the ghost of Parrington-Jackson, who refuses to rest until his murderer is caught.

*Go up the hill on Union Street and close to the top you will find the entrance to the Galleries Shopping Centre. Beside this entrance there is a multi-storey car park on which there is a stone plaque. This will be the subject of our next stop.*

## 3. Newgate Prison

Just outside of the Castle Park entrance to the Galleries, there is a plaque on the adjacent multi-storey car park which reveals the unlikely history of the spot on which it stands. This used to be the location of Newgate Prison - one of the most notorious prison's in the country.

Originally built in 1148, it was one of the first large-scale prisons to be built anywhere in Britain. In 1649 it was renovated and expanded to potentially become home to almost a thousand prisoners at a time.

Throughout its history, conditions were absolutely abysmal. The rights of inmates were never considered at this time, but even compared to other prisons of the age, Newgate stood out as one of the most inhumane.

Prisoners were given only a single piece of bread each day along with a tumbler of water. Many of the inmates died of malnutrition or from one of the many diseases that were rife throughout the institution. Though some of these criminals had been convicted of violent offences, almost half of them were simply debtors.

Far and away the most feared place in the entire prison was known as "The Pit". It was a small, mostly subterranean cell with only a single window placed high in the wall - and at foot-level to passing pedestrians - who were able to peer into the squalid conditions as a warning to always remain among the law-abiding.

There were no beds, just straw on the floor and a bucket in the corner served as a toilet - which was emptied infrequently. The cell was reserved for only the most serious offenders and could sometimes hold up to eight men at a time.

Conditions at the prison became so appalling that alms boxes were placed by charities outside its walls, so that sympathetic people could donate money to the inmates trapped inside. Soon the institution was the target of prison reform campaigners who sought to improve the manner in which the criminals were kept.

These campaigns were successful and following a report which claimed that the prison was so dangerously unsanitary even the wardens could not safely work there, a new prison - Bristol New Gaol was built in 1820 as a replacement. Conditions there were said to be a huge improvement.

Although Newgate Prison is long gone, it survives in written accounts which detail not just the terrible conditions of the prison itself, but also the inhumane ways in which we used to treat even the most trivial of criminals.

*Cross the road to Castle Park. The bombed and burned remains of St Peter's Church are unmistakable.*

## 4. St Peter's Church

Now little more than a burned-out shell on Castle Park, St Peter's Church stands as a memorial to the 1,299 civilians of Bristol who died during six huge raids on the city during WWII. The story of its own destruction, and that of the surrounding area, is a tale of one of the most dramatic nights in the city's history.

Castle Park was once a busy labyrinth of streets, with shops, houses and churches fighting for space along the old medieval roads that had once made up central Bristol. Many of the oldest buildings were made of wood and packed densely alongside one another. The autumn of 1940 had been exceptionally dry, conditions could not have been more perfect for an inferno - and the Germans knew it.

The night of the 24th of November was the not the first raid on the city, that had happened on the 2nd of November, but with over three weeks without an attack, the people of Bristol were beginning to think that the raid which had claimed a huge swathe of Old Town was a lone aberration and that they would not be bombed again.

The first sign that something was amiss came a little after 6.30pm. People around St Peter's Church saw white lights falling from the sky, which many simply put down to fireworks left over from Guy Fawkes night a couple of weeks before. This was not the case. Known as fairy lights, these were illuminating flares dropped by the lead plane in a squadron so that the city could be better seen by the bombers following closely behind.

Although the city was in blackout, there was no way to disguise Bristol's location, as the Luftwaffe used the reflection of the moon on the River Avon to trace a path.

The air raid siren sounded only a few seconds before the first bomb struck. Over the course of the next 45 minutes over 12,000 incendiary bombs were dropped across Bristol, along with 160 tons of high explosives.

The area which is now Castle Park was hit worse than anywhere else, and by 7.30pm, was an inferno. Those who first arrived on the scene soon realised there was nothing they could do to help, as the sheer heat of the flames meant they could not even approach the bomb-stricken area.

Many people escaped by jumping into the Avon and swimming, others recalled simply running through fire until they were no longer surrounded by flames. One of the most terrifying images that stayed with many witnesses was the sight of a silver river running out of the blaze and into the harbour. They did not know at the time, but this was the melted roof of St Peter's Church.

207 people were killed that night and by the end of the war, Bristol would be the fifth most bombed city in Britain. It was not just Old Town that was targeted but also Park Street and Redcliffe, with lone bombs being dropped seemingly randomly across Bristol.

Astonishingly, this blitz was not reported by the national papers for fear of it damaging morale and even the local press massively downplayed the devastation. Thomas Underwood, the Lord Mayor of Bristol, made a profoundly memorable statement when he said: "The city of churches has, in one night, become the city of ruins."

What is left of St Peters Church is now kept as a monument to those who died. A plaque bearing their names is placed over one of the entrances and makes for harrowing, but important, reading.

*At the rear of St Peter's Church, follow the hill downwards and look for an area in a sunken basin of ground. In it, you should see some unusual looking stone ruins. This will be our next stop.*

## 5. Bristol Castle

At the edge of Castle Park, where it meets Newgate, are some rather strange looking ruins. These were once part of the foundations of a castle keep which stood on this spot, and as hard as it may be to believe, the whole area was home to the largest Norman castle in England.

The original castle actually predated the city itself and was first recorded in the Domesday book of 1088. At this time it was a motte and bailey design, which meant it was mostly made of wood and surrounded by a stone wall.

About a century later it was converted to stone, a common practice with the old style castles of the time. At this point, the castle would have looked very much like any we see all across the country, with a central tower surrounded by protective barricades.

Over the following centuries, as Bristol grew as a significant port city, so did the castle, and by 1480 it had encompassed almost the entirety of what is now Castle Park.

Generations of noble families had lived here, but most of what we know about them has only been found through relics and artifacts unearthed during archaeological studies of the area. In the 1970s, one such study revealed the skeleton of a small monkey, which is thought that have lived in the 15th or 16th century and was likely kept as a pet.

By 1480, the castle was an impregnable fortress that now had a moat encircling it, formed by diverting the River Frome around its base. By the mid 16th century, it had started to look a bit shabby, with walls and turrets partly collapsed, as finances for its upkeep began to run dry.

It was not quite the end for the castle though, as during the Civil War it would be partially restored and serve as a local base for Royalist troops in an attempt to save the city from any attack by Roundheads.

Despite attempts to keep the city neutral during the conflict, Bristol was taken by both the Parliamentarians and the Royalists at different times. Following the conflict, the castle was seen as a reminder of the war and also as a potential location for an insurgence to be planned, so on the orders of Oliver Cromwell it was dismantled.

It was taken apart brick by brick, with much of the original castle being repurposed to build nearby homes.

Despite this, there are still some traces of the castle to be found - aside from the keep foundations. There is a section of castle wall along the harbour side of the park and a "sally port" nearby - which served as a kind of emergency exit in case the castle was ever under siege. At the Old Market entrance there is the only remaining building of the castle, which is believed to have been the entrance to an enormous dining hall at the heart of the castle grounds.

*We shall be going in search of the castle moat for the next stop. Head towards the harbour side of the park and follow the path which leads downhill to the left. When you reach a small footbridge there is a small section of waterway which snakes below and disappears through a tunnel. Try and get a glimpse of this tunnel, though it's quite hard to spot!*

## 6. The Underground Waterways

Never is it more evident that there's more to Bristol than meets the eye than when you consider the myriad of winding waterways which flow beneath our feet.

The oldest, and most significant of these, can be seen at the edge of Castle Park where it meets the harbour and a small bridge crosses a section of what looks like a river. Looking very carefully over the railings you should be able to spy a semi-circular opening in the wall where the water disappears into darkness.

What seems at first to be a little inlet, is actually a man-made and centuries old diversion of the river which was dug into a trench and then reinforced with bricks to act as a moat around Bristol Castle. It once encircled the entirety of what is now Castle Park and acted as an extra barrier against attack.

This moat was such a prominent feature of Bristol that if you look at the central shield of the city's crest, you will see a boat passing through the tunnel where the water flows. This image is also used as the official logo of Bristol City Council.

Though it's entirely covered over now, sections of the moat were still visible well into the 20th century, but as Bristol grew and as land within the city became limited, more and more of these sections were built over until the entire moat was hidden from view.

Covering over the moat also helped to alleviate one of the city's biggest problems too. For as long as Bristol has had cars it has had problems with traffic flow. The Floating Harbour and the New Cut as well as the Frome, Avon and Malago rivers have all meant that traffic has had to work around the many waterways which crisscross our city. There has never been a perfect solution to this problem but it's often said that the ingenious design of Cumberland Basin and Plimsoll Bridge is as close as we've ever got to one.

During the early years of the 20th century, however, the solution was to not only cover over the rivers in the city centre, but also to join them all up using overflow weirs and trenches so that at times of maximum tide, the excess of the entire water system could be unloaded into the New Cut and feeder canal, which would help prevent the city from flooding.

By the middle of the 20th century, almost all waterways in the central area of Bristol were now underground and roads and buildings stood over them. As a result, we have been left with a dizzying labyrinth of rivers which stretch for almost forty miles beneath our feet.

The section of the moat around Castle Park is no longer an isolated stretch of water. If you were to take a canoe through the opening that is featured on the Bristol Crest, you would find yourself weaving through miles of ancient and narrow tunnels beneath the streets and eventually see daylight again by St Augustine's Parade, where you would be behind a metal grate which is visible beside the ferry landing at Cascade Steps.

*The next location is one of those strange buildings where the closer you get to it, the worse view you have, as to really appreciate this bizarre structure you have to view it side on. Follow the harbour with Castle Park behind you and then take to steps on to Saint Phillip's Bridge. About halfway across you should be able to see the Cheese Lane Shot Tower, which is a very narrow, white structure overlooking the harbour.*

## 7. The Shot Tower

The Cheese Lane Shot Tower is certainly one of the most distinct buildings to be found around the harbour. As well as its bizarre appearance, this tower has a rather fascinating history.

The building was used to create lead shot - small metal spheres which could be fired from shotguns. In the structure at the top, metal was superheated and then dripped through small holes where it would fall all the way through the 120 ft tall tower and into cold water at the base. The molten lead would solidify into near perfectly spherical pellets in an instant.

The tower was built to replace the original shot tower which was built in 1782. Based on a patent by Bristol inventor William Watts, it was the first shot tower in the world. Before this method was discovered, lead shot was created by allowing a drop of molten lead to solidify before rolling it in more liquid metal. The results were somewhat haphazard and created malformed and imperfect pellets.

There is an oft-repeated legend as to how William Watts came to invent his original shot tower. The story goes that one night, while hopelessly drunk, Watts was attempting to walk home but accidentally fell asleep in the grounds of St Mary Redcliffe. While there he had a dream - or a vision - of his wife pouring molten metal through a colander from the top of St Mary Redcliffe steeple, and in his dream, he watched as the round lead hit the ground around where he lay.

This story is almost certainly not true, as it first appears many decades after his death, but however inspiration came to Watts, his invention was an immediate success and made the man a huge fortune in its first year of operation.

261

Watts sold his patent in 1790 and poured all of his money into constructing Windsor Terrace in Clifton. This gargantuan project would involve building 200ft tall foundations so that the row of houses could look out over the city. The project was a catastrophe for Watts, bankrupting him before even the foundations could be completed, and the financial ruin almost left him destitute. Windsor Terrace was later completed by private investors and though the grand structure is a remarkable sight towering over Hotwells, it is still nicknamed "Watts' Folly".

The original shot tower was demolished in 1960 to allow for widening of roads. His tower was not built where the present one stands, but in Redcliffe, where it took advantage of the Redcliffe Caves which allowed the molten lead an extra drop before plunging into the water.

The current tower was built in 1969 but was almost immediately rendered redundant. The Bliemeister method became the standard process soon after the tower's construction, which was able to create lead shot faster and cheaper, requiring a drop of only three feet. The Cheese Lane Shot Tower remains an unused but fascinating relic to one man and his ingenious, yet deadly, invention.

*Continue along Saint Phillip's Bridge and then follow the Counterslip onto Victoria Street. Head south until you see a church tower with an alarming lean...*

## 8. The Leaning Tower of Bristol

You only have to look at Temple Church to know that something is very strange about this place.

It is so named as the entire area surrounding it (known as Temple) was grassland, owned and maintained by the Knights Templar (a secretive and ancient religious order which can loosely be described as early Catholicism plus conspiracy theories.) The area itself was called the Templars Meadow and an abbreviated version of this is where we get Temple Meads.

The church began construction in the early 14th century and its tower was completed in 1460. At some point during construction, it seems the builders understood that something was going wrong and that the tower was leaning, as there has been an attempt to ready this alarming angle by building the top section off kilter with the rest of it.

The lean is caused by the soft ground on which it was built and the church has been nicknamed "The Leaning Tower of Bristol" for at least a century (the lean is only two degrees shy of its far more famous Pisa counterpart). Parishioners before WWII recall how on Sundays, before church services, the children would place unshelled nuts in a crack which ran the length of the tower, so that when the service had ended and the bells were rung, the whole tower would sway so much that the nuts would crack and they would have a snack for the walk home.

In 1788, it was the scene of one of the most extraordinary events in Bristol history. George Luskins, a tailor from Yatton, had been exhibiting strange behaviour for some time, including singing and shouting in an inhuman sounding voice and having seizures with alarming frequency. It was declared that the man was possessed by no less than seven demons and he was brought to Temple Church where seven Anglican and Methodist ministers (including Methodism founder, John Wesley) worked together to save the man's soul. If accounts are to be believed, the exorcism was a complete success and George Luskins returned to Yatton and normal life soon afterwards.

The church was destroyed by an incendiary bomb on the 24th of November, 1940 and has remained disused ever since, but this mysterious building had one more secret yet to share.

For many centuries it had been rumoured that the church was built over a 12th century circular Knights Templar chapel. These rumours were long disregarded as hokum but in the 1960s, a team of archaeologists were granted permission to excavate the grounds to see if there was any truth in the legend.

Just as the stories predicted, the foundations of a circular church dating back to the 12th century were buried down there, and if you visit Temple Church today, the outline of this building has been marked out in stone.

*We're heading back to Castle Park but I suggest that when you reach the Counterslip, you take a left down a walkway about half way along which will eventually take you to Castle Bridge - the handsome "S" shaped footbridge over the harbour. On the Castle Park side there is a small cluster of five white beech trees along the path, each with a plaque at its base. This will be our next stop on the walk.*

# 9. The Normandy Trees

Along the southern edge of Castle Park, just before you reach Castle Bridge, there is a row of five white beech trees, each bearing a plaque at its roots. Each of these plaques has a name on it. Utah, Omaha, Gold, Juno and Sword.

These are the names given to the five beaches involved in the Normandy Landings of WWII and this collection of trees is a memorial to the Bristolians who lost their lives in the conflict which is credited with turning the war in Europe around.

Beginning on the 6th of June, 1944, and following extensive training exercises for the operation in south Devon, the Normandy Landings would go on for five weeks in total. Initially led by the allied forces of the UK, America, Canada and Free France, other contingents soon joined in to create an army representing 13 nations to go up against the German troops.

The German forces were massively outnumbered but had a strategic advantage in already having claimed the land. What they had not anticipated, however, was how the allied forces had thrown every resource available into this conflict, understanding its significance in the war and countering the Nazis with a massive bombardment from land, air and sea.

Eventually the German armies were forced to retreat from the coast. This not only resulted in the balance of power being reversed across Europe but also hugely diminished the odds of an invasion of Britain.

The victory in this battle came at an enormous cost - about 120,000 deaths on both sides of the conflict and hundreds of thousands more injured. Of course, a subtle, though devastating consequence was the psychological effects of such harrowing warfare, which would leave wounds many of the young men would take to their graves.

This small memorial in Castle Park was planted in 1995 and ever since, an increasingly dwindling band of men who fought in the war meet twice annually to remember those who died and the enormous sacrifice made by so many during those years.

Nearby there are cherry trees, planted in 1986 in remembrance of those killed in the atomic blasts at Hiroshima and Nagasaki, as well as a plaque near the bombed ruins of St Peter's Church, which remembers the Bristol men who fought against fascism in the Spanish Civil war from 1936-39.

These memorials are informally referred to as the Peace Garden and the plot was chosen as Castle Park itself was once destroyed by warfare. It is kept not just as a memorial to those who died but also in the hope that one day, the world might be at peace.

*We're heading for the final stop on this tour and this book. Follow the footpath west to the corner which meets High Street. On your right there is a concreted area in which an almost pyramid-like structure juts out of the ground. This is the subject of our last stop.*

## 10. The Medieval Vaults

On the barren, somewhat grim stretch of concrete between Castle Park and High Street is an odd little structure made of cement blocks.

This was a somewhat hasty solution to a post-war problem, which still hasn't been resolved to this day.

The area surrounding this structure was once inside a large Tudor house. Like most buildings in the area, it was timber framed and therefore incinerated in the 1940 Luftwaffe strike.

Once the flames were extinguished and the ash cleared away, a hole in the ground was revealed, inside of which were a pair of 14th century storage vaults.

These medieval vaults were once the basement of the Tudor house and had been built to store food and wine.

Now completely exposed, the basement was covered over with wooden boards until the war was over, and after that, the rather ugly encasement you see today was built over it - with a promise that something more pleasing to the eye would eventually replace it.

Unfortunately, the vaults are very inaccessible and are infrequently opened, but there's something quite fascinating about knowing they're down there - an extraordinary and historic treasure buried just out of sight.

The plans to replace the opening to the vaults may never have materialised, but in a way the grey and sombre looking structure encapsulates everything I love about Weird Bristol. It is these odd bits of the city which might catch your eye but be forgotten as soon as you've passed them. It has been my privilege to share some of these odd little facts about our wonderful city and I hope it has encouraged you to start exploring and search out some weird history for yourself!

*So that concludes our tour. Or does it? If you look across the Road to St Nicholas Street you will find a drinking fountain featuring the likeness of Queen Victoria. If you go there, you will find yourself on the first page of the first walk in the book...*

## About The Author

Charlie Revelle-Smith was born in Essex and raised in Cornwall but in the year 2000, he moved to Bristol to study English at the University of the West of England.

He learned a lot over those three years at university, most significantly, how much he loved his adopted home.

Now regarding himself as a "Naturalised Bristolian" Charlie spends a good portion of his life wandering around the streets of Bristol, often accompanied by his dog Reggie, in search of oddities for his popular Twitter feed and Instagram account @WeirdBristol, which documents the lesser known and hidden history of the city.

The *Weird Bristol* book is Charlie's first non-fiction book after writing several successful novels (and a few unsuccessful ones!) Many of his novels are historic mysteries, mostly set during the Victorian era and early 20th century, but from 2015-18 he published *The Bristol Murders* series which are set in contemporary Bristol.

Printed in Great
Britain
by Amazon